Best Easy Day Hikes
Glacier and Waterton Lakes National Parks

Help Us Keep This Guide Up to Date

Every effort has been made by the author and editors to make this guide as accurate and useful as possible. However, many things can change after a guide is published—trails are rerouted, regulations change, techniques evolve, facilities come under new management, etc.

We would love to hear from you concerning your experiences with this guide and how you feel it could be improved and kept up to date. While we may not be able to respond to all comments and suggestions, we'll take them to heart and we'll also make certain to share them with the author. Please send your comments and suggestions to the following address:

The Globe Pequot Press
Reader Response/Editorial Department
P.O. Box 480
Guilford, CT 06437

Or you may e-mail us at:

editorial@GlobePequot.com

Thanks for your input, and happy trails!

Best Easy Day Hikes Series

Best Easy Day Hikes Glacier and Waterton Lakes National Parks

Second Edition

Erik Molvar

GUILFORD, CONNECTICUT
HELENA, MONTANA
AN IMPRINT OF THE GLOBE PEQUOT PRESS

FALCONGUIDES®

Copyright © 1998, 2007 Morris Book Publishing, LLC

ALL RIGHTS RESERVED. No part of this book may be reproduced or transmitted in any form by any means, electronic or mechanical, including photocopying and recording, or by any information storage and retrieval system, except as, may be expressly permitted in writing from the publisher. Requests for permission should be addressed to The Globe Pequot Press, Attn: Rights and Permission Department, P.O. Box 480, Guilford, CT 06437.

Falcon and FalconGuides are registered trademarks of Morris Book Publishing, LLC.

Maps by Mapping Specialists. © Morris Book Publishing, LLC

Library of Congress Cataloging-in-Publication Data is available.
ISBN-13: 978-0-7627-3633-1

Manufactured in the United States of America
Second Edition/Fourth Printing

Contents

Acknowledgments

This guide would not have been possible without the years of excellent service put in by the rangers with whom I had the pleasure of dealing. I would like to thank Mr. Jack Potter, GNP Chief of Science and Resource Management, for his editorial input throughout the writing of this book. I also thank Nancy Hoffman and Tom Habecker, former Glacier rangers, for their helpful comments and suggestions concerning the guide. Clyde Lockwood of the Glacier Natural History Association provided the initial assistance in dealing with publishing firms, and I am grateful for his continued support of my efforts. Randall Schwanke, Locke Marshall, Bill Thorpe, and Chrisy Gustavison of Waterton Lakes National Park provided editorial assistance for the Canadian hikes. Thanks to Renelle Jacobsen for her hospitality and friendship. And thanks to Little Joe Manley just for being himself.

Introduction

What's a "best easy" hike?

Our national parks and forests serve as windows to the natural world, reservoirs of natural beauty and grandeur, and wellsprings of inspiration. As such, they are magnets to people who seek to reestablish their ties with nature, learn more about the world in which we live, or simply find a quiet escape from the hustle and bustle of modern society. Glacier National Park and its Canadian neighbor, Waterton Lakes National Park, feature mountain fastnesses clad in glaciers, azure lakes, and sparkling waterfalls, inviting the visitor to step into the natural world.

Anyone who travels widely in these areas will soon notice that park visitors fall into two distinct categories—those who want to immerse themselves in wilderness backcountry for several days at a time, and those who have only a day or two and would like a choice sampling of the area's special features. This book is for the second group.

I gathered materials for this guide as I researched the much larger and more comprehensive *Hiking Glacier and Waterton Lakes National Parks*. That book covers every trail in both parks, including those that are neither best nor easy. *Best Easy Day Hikes Glacier and Waterton Lakes* includes only short, less strenuous hikes that showcase the best features of the region.

These hikes vary in length, but most are short. Most lack big hills, and the few long grades that appear in this book can be tackled in a leisurely fashion. All hikes are on easy-to-follow trails with no off-trail route-finding challenges.

Trailhead access is easy for all hikes, and you can reach any of these trailheads with a low-clearance passenger car.

Some of the hikes in this book might not seem easy to some, but they will be easy for others. To help you decide what trails are right for you, I've ranked the hikes from easiest to more challenging on the next page. Please keep in mind that long does not always equal difficult. Other factors, such as elevation gain and trail conditions, have to be considered.

I hope you thoroughly enjoy your "best easy" hiking through the natural wonders of Glacier and Waterton Lakes National Parks.

Ranking the Hikes

The following list ranks the hikes in this book from easiest to more challenging:

Trail of the Cedars, Hike 5 *8/24/13* *8/25/13*
Swiftcurrent Nature Trail, Hike 18
Running Eagle Falls, Hike 12
Blakiston Falls, Hike 28
Rainbow Falls, Hike 24
Cameron Lake, Hike 26
Sun Point Nature Trail, Hike 10
Kootenai Lakes, Hike 25
Beaver Pond Trail, Hike 11
Bullhead Lake, Hike 21
Johns Lake Loop, Hike 3
McDonald Creek, Hike 4
Grinnell Lake, Hike 19 *8/25/13 Via boat*
McDonald Lake Trail, Hike 2
Bowman Lake, Hike 1
Lower Bertha Falls, Hike 23
St. Mary and Virginia Falls, Hike 9 *8/26/13*
Upper Two Medicine Lake, Hike 16
Avalanche Lake, Hike 6
Appistoki Falls, Hike 13
Hidden Lake, Hike 7 *8/24/13 to LookOut*
Two Medicine Lake, Hike 14
Bears Hump, Hike 22
Aster Park, Hike 15
Lineham Falls, Hike 27
Haystack Butte, Hike 8
Iceberg Lake, Hike 20
Apikuni Falls, Hike 17

Zero Impact

Traveling in a national park such as Glacier is like visiting a famous museum. You obviously don't want to leave your mark on an art treasure. If everybody who visited the museum left one tiny mark, the piece of art would be destroyed—and what would a big building full of trashed art be worth? The same goes for pristine wilderness such as that found in the Northern Rockies. If we all left just one little mark on the landscape, the wilderness would soon be despoiled.

A wilderness can accommodate plenty of human use as long as everybody treats it with respect. But a few thoughtless or uninformed visitors can ruin it for everyone who follows. And the need for good manners applies to all wilderness visitors, not just backpackers. Day hikers should also adhere strictly to "zero impact" principles. We all must pass through the landscape respectfully, leaving no clues that we have gone before.

Three FalconGuide Principles of Zero Impact

- Leave with everything you brought with you.
- Leave no sign of your visit.
- Leave the landscape as you found it.

Most of us know better than to litter, in or out of the wilderness. Even the tiniest scrap of paper left along the trail or at a campsite detracts from the landscape's pristine character. This means that you should pack out everything, even biodegradable items such as orange peels, which can take years to decompose. It's also a good idea to pick up any trash that less considerate hikers have left behind.

To avoid damaging the trailside soil and plants, stay on the main path. Avoid cutting switchbacks and venturing onto fragile vegetation. When taking a rest stop, select a durable surface like a bare log, rock, or sandy beach. Don't pick up "souvenirs," such as rocks, antlers, feathers, or wildflowers. The next person wants to discover them, too, and taking such souvenirs violates park regulations.

Avoid making loud noises that disturb the silence others may be enjoying. Remember, sound travels easily in the outdoors. Be courteous. When nature calls, use established outhouse facilities whenever possible. If these are unavailable, bury human waste 6 to 8 inches deep and pack out used toilet paper. This is a good reason to carry a lightweight trowel. Keep wastes at least 300 feet away from any surface water or boggy spots.

Finally, and perhaps most importantly, strictly follow the pack-it-in/pack-it-out rule. If you carry something into the wilderness, consume it completely or carry it out with you. Zero impact—put your ear to the ground in the wilderness and listen carefully. The thousands of people coming behind you are thanking you for your courtesy and good sense.

Hiking with Kids

Hiking with children can be one of the most rewarding and memorable experiences a family can undertake. Hiking offers a tremendous learning opportunity, giving children confidence and a growing awareness of the world around them. Kids can enrich the hiking experiences of their parents as well, since they often find beauty in small details that adults overlook.

Choose a destination that is accessible to your kids, and set your goals with your youngest child's abilities in mind. If you are carrying a young child in a kid-carrier backpack, you may be able to travel farther than you could if that child were walking. Young children can surprise you with their ability to travel long distances, if parents are willing to shoulder some of the extra load.

As a general rule, children two to four years old can be expected to walk up to 2 miles per day, taking rest stops every ten to fifteen minutes. Children five to seven years of age can usually hike up to 4 miles per day, and should rest every thirty to forty-five minutes. Once children reach eight or nine years of age, they can be expected to cover up to 7 miles a day.

Start with short trips so the kids can get accustomed to hiking uneven trails. Children tire quickly and are easily distracted, so don't be surprised if you don't make it to your destination. Stay flexible and consider alternate turnaround points en route to your goal. Point out special sights, sounds, and smells along the way to help your children enjoy the trip and learn about what they see. If you make the hike fun, keeping the kids interested, they will keep going.

Careful planning with an emphasis on safety will help make your trip an enjoyable one. Allow older children to carry their own packs, and perhaps bring a favorite toy or book along. These things, along with some equipment kids can carry, help develop a sense of responsibility and teach young hikers the advantages of packing light. Children over age four can carry a day pack, but parents should be prepared to carry the pack for a tired child. Limit the weight of an older child's pack to 20 percent of the child's body weight. Parents may have to carry some of the child's gear.

Young skin is very sensitive to the sun and to insect bites. Apply sunscreen to your kids before and during the trip. Carry a good insect repellant, preferably a natural product, and apply it as necessary. Also consider carrying a product that takes the itch out of insect bites. A hat helps keep bright sun out of sensitive young eyes. Rain gear is always an important consideration in the mountains, since storms and cold weather tend to move in unexpectedly. Kids seem to have less tolerance to cold than adults, so bring ample warm clothing. If your hike will take you to the edge of a river or lake, careful supervision of your kids is a must. Consider bringing a life vest for your child.

Parents should be aware that both grizzly bears and mountain lions range throughout the park. Make sure that your group stays together, and do not let children run ahead.

Among your important considerations when hiking with children should be the wilderness experience of other hikers. Kids are naturally inclined to run around, chase animals, collect flowers and rocks, and shatter the silence with their screams. These behaviors may be fine in town, but they are inappropriate in a wilderness setting. Always be aware that many visitors who seek out the wild country of Glacier do so to find tranquillity and solitude. Supervise your children so that their actions do not impose on others. Finally, since children learn by example, day hiking offers an excellent opportunity to instruct children in the arts of treading lightly and reducing their impact on the landscape.

Map Legend

–··–··–	International boundary	**24**	Trail start
–·–·–	Park boundary	🏃	Interpretive Trail
2	U.S. highway	♿	Wheelchair-accessible
49	State highway	▲	Developed campground
486	Primary road	△	Undeveloped campground
	Other road	▲	Backcountry campground
▬▬▬▬	Featured trail	🧍	Ranger station
- - - - -	Other trail	⛵	Boat Launch
⊢––⊢––⊢	Railroad	❓	Visitor center
• • • • •	Continental Divide	⊼	Picnic area
‿	Pass	🍴	Food and lodging
▲	Spot elevation	🐎	Riding stable
⌒⌒	Intermittent stream	⚓	Boat dock
//	Falls	🗼	Lookout
◗	Lake	👁	Overlook
◗	Glacier	⚒	Mine
•	Point of interest	🛏	Lodging
○	Town	◨	Shelter

Lake McDonald, near the west entrance of Glacier National Park, is the largest body of water in the park. It is 10 miles long and has a maximum depth of 472 feet. The lakebed was carved out by a huge glacier that filled the entire valley, leaving a characteristic U-shaped basin. Lake McDonald was once fair fishing for native cutthroat trout, but ever since the introduction of lake trout decimated the native populations of cutthroat and bull trout, the lake has offered very poor fishing. At the lake's foot lie the low foothills of the Apgar Range and the Belton Hills, while snowcapped peaks along the Continental Divide loom to the east of the lake's head. The country is characterized by low, east–west ridges rising to rugged peaks. Dense forests cover the eastern shore of the lake, grading from cedars, birches, and larches at lower elevations to Douglas firs and lodgepole pines higher up. The western shore and the Apgar Mountains show dramatic evidence of the 2003 Robert Fire.

The North Fork of the Flathead River occupies a forested valley bounded on the west by the Whitefish Range and on the east by the craggy Livingston Range. The climate here reflects a maritime influence, with storm fronts pushing in from the Pacific Ocean. As a result, the North Fork country gets quite a bit of precipitation over the course of a year, most of which falls in wintertime as snow. Lodgepole pines dominate the vegetation of the valley floor, dependent on periodic fires to maintain their competitive edge over more shade-tolerant species. The serotinous cones of lodgepoles are covered with resin that melts and allows the cone to release seeds only in the presence of heat provided by forest fires. The seeds then fall on fertile soil in openings created by the fire, where they germinate and thrive in direct sunlight. Many fires have burned along the North Fork of the Flathead River during the last several decades, leaving their mark on the forest.

Hikes around Lake McDonald and the North Fork tend to pass through heavy forest, with limited opportunities for sweeping views. Burns and lakes provide occasional vistas. The forest itself abounds with wild berries in late summer. Lakes and streams typically harbor native westslope cutthroat trout, though rainbow trout were introduced in some areas. In general, the lakes provide much better fishing than the streams, which are so pure that they contain few nutrients to sustain a productive food web. Know the park fishing regulations, and check for closures and catch limits before you set out.

Wildlife in this part of Glacier reflects the boreal nature of the region, with elk and white-tailed deer being plentiful. Taiga species, such as lynx and fisher, are occasionally seen in thick stands of lodgepole pine at lower elevations. The North Fork country is home to several active wolf packs, which colonized the park naturally from Canada. Hikers who see tracks or hear the howl of these endangered predators can consider themselves truly fortunate. Birders will find the large glacial lakes of this area good places to see ospreys, bald eagles, and common loons.

West Glacier, Montana, is the western gateway to the park and serves as trailhead and rafting hub for that side of the park. Vendors offer a wide variety of tourist services at West Glacier, Apgar Village, and Lake McDonald Lodge, including guided horse trips, gas, restaurants, and lodging. Major car campgrounds are located at Apgar and Avalanche Creek; these tend to be crowded and noisy. A quieter tents-only campground is located on Sprague Creek near Lake McDonald Lodge.

The North Fork Valley can be accessed via the Inside North Fork Road (Glacier Route 7), a narrow gravel road that runs along the river inside the park boundary. There are auto campgrounds at Quartz and Logging Creeks along the way, as well as campgrounds at the foot of Bowman and Kintla Lakes. An alternate route into the North Fork area is the Polebridge Road, which can be accessed from the terminus of the Camas Road or from the town of Columbia Falls, Montana, and runs 16 miles north to the settlement of Polebridge. This road, heavily traveled by logging trucks, is frequently in rough condition. Polebridge is an authentic frontier community, serving a handful of homesteads and ranches on the west bank of the river. This "town" boasts a mercantile store selling gas and groceries and the Northern Lights Saloon, which serves meals and libations to weary travelers in an atmosphere of down-home hospitality. Just north of this quaint community, a new two-lane bridge crosses the river to link up with Glacier Route 7.

1 Bowman Lake

Type of hike: Out-and-back
Total distance: Up to 14.2 miles (22.9 km) round-trip

Time required: 1 to 9 hours, depending on length of hike
Elevation change: Minimal

Finding the trailhead: Follow Glacier Route 7 north to its junction with Bowman Lake Road, just north of Polebridge. Take Bowman Lake Road (a narrow but graded gravel road) to its terminus at Bowman Campground. The trail departs from the northeast corner of the campground, near the lakeshore.

The Hike

This trail follows the northwestern shore of Bowman Lake for 7 miles of gentle up-and-down hiking. Use it as a back-pack route in itself or as a day hike of any length. The trail winds past Bowman Lake before ascending a U-shaped valley carved by a glacier between rugged peaks. Views across the lake include the glacier-carved summits of Square Peak, Rainbow Peak, and Mount Carter. The lake is prime osprey and bald eagle habitat and is often closed to boating, fishing, and hiking above the upper campground to protect active eagle nests. Loons are frequently sighted on the lake's surface. The backcountry campsite near the head of the lake is popular with hikers and boaters alike.

Key Points

- **0.0** Trail sign. Trail follows shore of Bowman Lake.
- **0.7** Junction with Numa Ridge Lookout Trail. Stay right.
- **7.1** Campground at head of Bowman Lake.
- **14.2** Return to trailhead.

Bowman Lake

RF 1:177,500

N

Hypsometry

| Elevation (feet) |
| 10,000 |
| 9,000 |
| 8,000 |
| 7,000 |
| 6,000 |
| 5,000 |
| 4,000 |
| 3,000 |

Kilometers 0 — 4
Miles 0 — 4

Weasel Collar Glacier

Carter Glacier

Continental Divide

Mount Carter 9843 ft 3000 m

Rainbow Glacier

Cerulean Lake

Square Peak 8777 ft 2675 m

Cerulean Ridge

Vulture Peak 9638 ft 2937 m

Vulture Glacier

Bowman Lake Trail

Bowman Lake

Quartz Lake

Logging Ridge

Numa

Akokala Lake

Middle Quartz Lake

Lower Quartz Lake

Quartz Ridge

Bowman Lake

Bowman Creek

Bowman Lake Road

Akokala Creek

Teepee Flat

Big Prairie

Glacier Route 7

Road Closed in Winter

486

2 McDonald Lake Trail

Type of hike: Shuttle
Total distance: 6.6 miles
(10.6 km) one way

Time required: 3 to 5 hours
Elevation change: 160-foot gain
and loss

Finding the trailhead: From Apgar, follow the Camas Road north for 0.8 mile and turn right at the sign for Fish Creek Campground. Follow the Inside North Fork Road past the campground ranger station. As the road turns to gravel, look for a road information sign with a parking area a short distance beyond it on the left-hand side. Park here; the hike begins on the opposite side of the road.

The Hike

This relatively obscure and lightly traveled trail follows the roadless northwestern shore of Lake McDonald. Most of the trail is within forest that burned in a hot fire in 2003, with frequent views through the charred snags of the surrounding mountain scenery. Hikers seeking a shorter trip can start at the west end and visit Rocky Point (1.6 miles round-trip), or start from the eastern end of the trail and hike to the Lake McDonald backcountry camp (4.4 miles round-trip).

After crossing a bridge over Fern Creek, the trail runs through a young forest of lodgepole pine underlain by beargrass. This forest community is typical of postfire coniferous forests in northwestern Montana. The path soon meets a broad trail that begins in the Fish Creek Campground. Follow this wide avenue northeast along the lakeshore to reach a junction with the side trail that runs to a headland known as Rocky Point. This side trip is well worth the effort, and ends on an outcrop with superb views

McDonald Lake Trail

RF 1:177,500

N

Kilometers
0   4

Miles
0   4

Hypsometry

Elevation (feet)

10,000
9,000
8,000
7,000
6,000
5,000
4,000
3,000

UTM Zone 11 | UTM Zone 12

McGee Creek

Camas Road

Fish Creek

Fern Creek

Howe Lake

Howe Ridge

Fish Creek

Lake McDonald Trail

Lake McDonald

Going-to-the-Sun Road

Apgar

John F. Stevens Canyon

Snyder Ridge

Lincoln Creek

Lincoln Lake Trail

Sprague Creek

Fish Lake Trail

Mt. Brown Lookout Tr.

Snyder Lake Trail

Snyder Lakes

Sperry Chalet

Sperry Glacier

Lincoln Lake

McDonald Falls

Sprague Creek

Fish Lake

5390000

5380000

720000

780000

290000

up Lake McDonald. The sharp crags above the lake's head are, from left to right, Mount Brown, the Little Matterhorn, Edwards Peak, Gunsight Mountain, and Mount Jackson.

The Lake McDonald Trail makes a stiff climb inland, entering country that burned in 1929 and again during the dry summer of 2003. Young trees grow densely here, competing to become the next dominant members of the forest overstory. The path next emerges from the forest at a pebble beach at mile 1.8; here, Mount Cannon can be seen along with the summits mentioned above. The trail runs close to the shoreline now, revealing glimpses of the turquoise water through the charred snags.

At mile 4.6, a spur trail descends to the Lake McDonald backcountry camp (abandoned after the 2003 fire), which is situated on a small point. You can look both up and down Lake McDonald from the beach gravels of this point, with views all the way up the McDonald Creek Valley to the Garden Wall. Mounts Stanton and Vaught can now be seen above the north side of the lake.

The main trail continues through the burned forest, swinging inland shortly before joining an old dirt road. The hike follows this route to reach the eastern trailhead at the end of the North Shore Road.

Key Points

- **0.0** Trailhead on North Fork Road.
- **0.1** Trail crosses Fern Creek.
- **0.4** Junction with trail from Fish Creek Campground. Bear left.
- **0.5** Junction with Rocky Point spur trail (0.3 mile).
- **4.6** Spur trail descends to now-abandoned Lake McDonald camp (0.2 mile).
- **6.6** Trail reaches end of North Shore Road.

3 Johns Lake Loop

Type of hike: Loop or shuttle
Total distance: 2.4 miles
(3.9 km)

Time required: 1 to 2 hours
Elevation change: 100-foot gain
and loss

Finding the trailhead: Follow Going-to-the-Sun Road northeast from Lake McDonald Lodge for 1.5 miles. Park at the Johns Lake Trailhead on the right side of the road, just before the junction with the North Shore Road.

The Hike

This popular loop runs through the forest above the head of Lake McDonald, visiting a woodland lake as well as Sacred Dancing Cascade and McDonald Falls along McDonald Creek. Parts of the trail receive heavy horse use from trail rides that originate at Lake McDonald Lodge.

The hike begins with a moderate climb into the cedar-hemlock forest south of Going-to-the-Sun Road. Turn left at the first junction as the trail rises into an old burn populated by Douglas fir and lodgepole pine. Beargrass and huckleberry thrive in the sunny understory found here. Follow the signs for Johns Lake as the path returns to the closed-canopy forest. The path reaches Johns Lake 0.2 mile later. This shallow pool in the woodlands reflects the summits of Mounts Stanton and Vaught.

A connecting trail runs northward from the lakeshore toward Avalanche Lake; avoid it in favor of the wider path bound for Going-to-the-Sun Road. This trail descends through the deep shade of western hemlocks, and a carpet of moss covers the forest floor. Upon reaching the road,

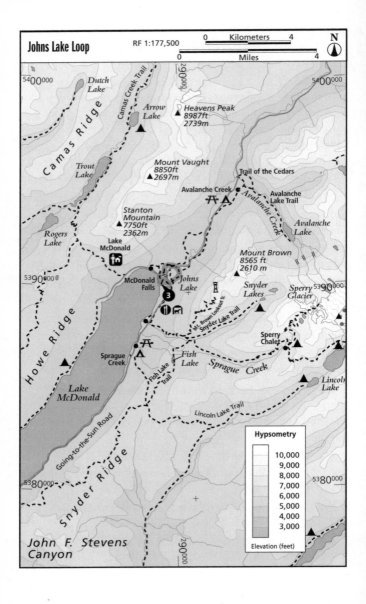

Johns Lake Loop

RF 1:177,500

Kilometers
0   4

Miles
0   4

N

5400000

Dutch Lake

Camas Ridge

Camas Creek Trail

Arrow Lake

Heavens Peak
8987ft
2739m

5400000

Mount Vaught
8850ft
2697m

Trail of the Cedars

Trout Lake

Avalanche Creek

Avalanche Lake Trail

Avalanche Creek

Avalanche Lake

Stanton Mountain
7750ft
2362m

Rogers Lake

Lake McDonald

Mount Brown
8565 ft
2610 m

Snyder Lakes

Sperry Glacier

5390000

McDonald Falls

Johns Lake

3

Mt. Brown Lookout Tr.

Snyder Lake Trail

5390000

Howe Ridge

Sprague Creek

Fish Lake Trail

Fish Lake

Sprague Creek

Sperry Chalet

Lincoln Lake

Lake McDonald

Going-to-the-Sun Road

Lincoln Lake Trail

Snyder Ridge

5380000

Hypsometry

10,000
9,000
8,000
7,000
6,000
5,000
4,000
3,000

Elevation (feet)

5380000

John F. Stevens Canyon

2900000

cross the crosswalk and turn right (north) to reach the paved pathway that descends to Sacred Dancing Cascade. Cross McDonald Creek on the bridge just below a stairstep waterfall.

On the far bank, turn left (south) and choose the primitive path with the "no horses" sign. This path follows the rims of low cliffs that guard McDonald Creek, with fine views of riffled white water and turquoise pools. The path soon reaches McDonald Falls, and a spur track runs to the lip where water plunges as a thundering cataract. The trail then wanders through a bottomland hemlock forest to reach the North Shore Road. Shuttle hikers should turn right on this road to reach the McDonald Creek Trailhead; loop hikers turn left, crossing the road bridge and then following a horse trail back to the Johns Lake Trailhead. During wet weather, stick to the road to avoid horse-churned mud.

Key Points

0.0	Johns Lake Trailhead.
0.2	Trail joins McDonald horse trail. Turn left.
0.7	Johns Lake Trail splits away from horse loop. Turn right.
0.9	Johns Lake. Junction with McDonald Creek Trail. Turn left.
1.1	Trail crosses Going-to-the-Sun Road. Bear right on road to link with Sacred Dancing Cascade access ramp.
1.2	Bridge over McDonald Creek.
1.3	Junction with McDonald Creek Trail. Turn left, then left again onto primitive stream bank trail (marked "no horses").
1.5	McDonald Falls.
2.1	Trail emerges on North Shore Road. Turn left to complete loop.
2.4	Johns Lake Trailhead.

4 McDonald Creek

Type of hike: Out-and-back
Total distance: 6.8-miles
(10.9 km) round-trip

Time required: 3 to 5 hours
Elevation change: 200-foot gain

Finding the trailhead: From Lake McDonald Lodge, follow Going-to-the-Sun Road northeast for several miles to the junction with the North Shore Road. Turn left, crossing the bridge over McDonald Creek to reach the marked trailhead on the right side of the road.

The Hike

This short hike follows a fragment of the old packers' trail that ran up the McDonald Creek Valley before Going-to-the-Sun Road was built. Here McDonald Creek is guarded by the low walls of a distinctive little gorge, its aquamarine waters flow down as rushing waterfalls and quiet runs. Part of the trail is used for trail rides originating at Lake McDonald Lodge, so be prepared to meet horses along the way. The hike is particularly striking in the silence of early winter, when massive icicles hang from the walls of the gorge.

The trail begins by wandering northwest through a mixed woodland of hemlock, larch, and Douglas fir occupying the bottomlands along McDonald Creek. After a short journey, the path approaches the stream, with its turquoise waters swirling down between slanted slabs of stone. To view the roaring cataract of McDonald Falls, take a short side trip down the stream bank on an unofficial trail marked with a "no horses" sign. The main path now runs northeast along the rim of a small gorge. The crenelated facade of Mount Brown looms across the valley, a constant presence along this portion of the route. The path soon reaches the sturdy bridge over Sacred Dancing Cascade, and just upstream the water descends gracefully across a lengthy series of tiny stairsteps.

The wider path leads across the stream to a parking area and beyond to Johns Lake; the narrow gravel pathway, McDonald Creek Trail, continues upstream along the north bank of the creek. After passing a small waterfall, the trail turns inland to enter the silent hallways of climax coniferous forest. Where it next emerges, streamside, the waters glide placidly through cedar bottoms. The lofty edifice of Mount Cannon rises ahead, and soon Mount Vaught and Heavens Peak appear on the north side of the valley. Watch for moose as well as beaver, which have dammed some of the slow-moving backwaters in this area.

The path then wanders inland, passing through a deep forest of hemlock. At mile 2.2, the horse tours turn around at a wide spot in the timber. A more primitive path continues onward, becoming overgrown with low brush for a short stretch. It soon crosses a gravelly wash where floodwaters from the slopes of Mount Vaught have buried the tree trunks in rocky debris. On the far side of the stream course, the path improves for a long sojourn through hemlock forest. Travelers are rewarded as the trail emerges beside the rocky upper gorge of McDonald Creek. Here, waters churn over violent waterfalls, and the imposing summit of Mount Cannon rises regally above the stream. Watch your step; there are no guardrails here to prevent a tumble into the churning white water. The path ends suddenly atop the bedrock with views of a particularly impressive falls.

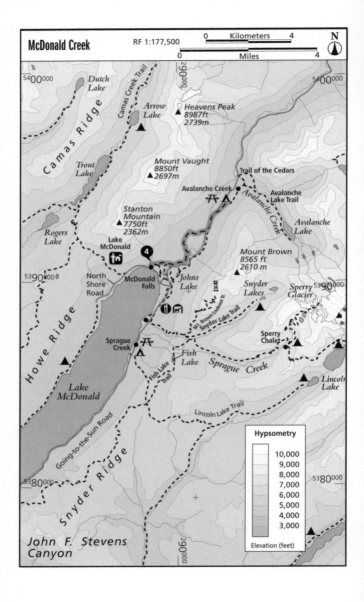

McDonald Creek

RF 1:177,500

Kilometers 0 — 4

Miles 0 — 4

N

5400000

290000

5400000

Dutch Lake

Camas Creek Trail

Camas Ridge

Arrow Lake

Heavens Peak 8987ft 2739m

Mount Vaught 8850ft 2697m

Trail of the Cedars

Avalanche Creek

Avalanche Lake Trail

Trout Lake

Stanton Mountain 7750ft 2362m

Avalanche Creek

Avalanche Lake

Rogers Lake

Lake McDonald

4

Mount Brown 8565 ft 2610 m

Snyder Lakes

Sperry Glacier

5390000

North Shore Road

McDonald Falls

Johns Lake

Mt Brown Lookout Tr.

Snyder Lake Trail

5390000

Howe Ridge

Sprague Creek

Fish Lake

Fish Lake Trail

Sprague Creek

Sperry Chalet

Lincoln Lake

Lake McDonald

Going-to-the-Sun Road

Lincoln Lake Trail

5380000

290000

5380000

Hypsometry	
	10,000
	9,000
	8,000
	7,000
	6,000
	5,000
	4,000
	3,000

Elevation (feet)

Snyder Ridge

John F. Stevens Canyon

Key Points

0.0 North Shore Road.

0.9 Bridge over McDonald Creek. Stay on north bank of creek.

2.2 Horse turnaround point.

3.4 Trail ends at edge of gorge.

6.8 Return to trailhead.

5 Trail of the Cedars

Type of hike: Loop
Total distance: 0.7 mile (1.1 km)

Time required: 20 to 60 minutes
Elevation change: Minimal

Finding the trailhead: Trail of the Cedars Trailhead, across from Avalanche Picnic Area on Going-to-the-Sun Road.

The Hike

This self-guiding nature trail forms a semi-loop through old-growth forest in the bottoms of Avalanche Creek. Avalanche Gorge lies at the apex of the loop, with swirling waters and sculpted argillite walls. The northern leg of the trail follows a boardwalk, while the southern leg is paved, with benches along the way so hikers can stop and enjoy the grandeur of the forest. The entire loop is wheelchair accessible. The trailhead is about 0.3 mile from the parking lot.

From the trailhead, follow the boardwalk that runs through the forest north of Avalanche Creek. The old growth that rises from these damp and fertile bottoms has remained undisturbed for centuries, and the trees have grown tall and stout in the absence of fire and avalanche. The oldest trees are western red cedar and black cottonwood, species more commonly found along coastal rivers of the Pacific Northwest. Ferns and devil's club occupy the understory. Most of the younger trees are western hemlock, which can be identified by its drooping treetop leader. It is the most shade-tolerant of Glacier's conifers, and its seedlings can thrive beneath a closed-canopy forest where those of other species cannot.

Note the diversity of tree sizes and ages. As the oldest trees succumb to disease and fall to the forest floor, they create sunny gaps in the canopy so that light can reach the ground and allow new seedlings to take root. Over the span of centuries, this gradual replacement of the stand results in a broad diversity of tree heights, forming a multilayered canopy that offers a multitude of ecological niches for forest creatures with specialized diets and food-gathering techniques—such forest dwellers as birds, voles, and squirrels. It is this diversity of plant and animal life that makes old-growth forest so valuable from an ecological standpoint.

As it makes its way through the forest, the boardwalk passes a mossy outcrop of stone. Water seeps constantly from the fissures in this rock, and in winter great stalactites of ice form here. The path then crosses a bridge at the mouth of Avalanche Gorge, where water has carved a deep and whorled channel into the argillite. Moss grows thick at the edges of the gorge, thriving in the constant mist provided by a waterfall just upstream. Watch for a small gray bird known as the water ouzel, which nests behind waterfalls and makes frequent dives into the current in a quest for aquatic insects.

On the far bank of the creek, a paved path leads westward, following Avalanche Creek as it passes through an abandoned loop of the Avalanche Creek Campground. Note

Trail of the Cedars

RF 1:177,500

Kilometers 0 — 4

Miles 0 — 4

N

Lake Evangeline

McDonald Creek

The Loop

The Salamander Glacier

Garden Wall

Camas Lake

Haystack Butte

Weeping Wall

Camas Creek Trail

54 00 000

Arrow Lake

Heavens Peak 8987ft 2739m

Triple Arches

Mount Oberlin 8180ft 2493m

Mount Clements 8760 ft 2670 m

Logan Pass

Mount Vaught 8850ft 2697m

5 Trail of the Cedars

Avalanche Creek

Avalanche Lake Trail

Hidden Lake

Stanton Mountain 7750ft 2362m

Avalanche Creek

Avalanche Lake

Continental Divide

Lake McDonald

53 90 000

McDonald Falls

Johns Lake

Mount Brown 8565 ft 2610 m

Snyder Lakes

Sperry Glacier

Gunsight Mountain 9258 ft 2821 m

53 90 000

Lake McDonald

Mt. Brown Lookout Tr.

Snyder Lake Trail

Sperry Chalet

Sprague Creek

Fish Lake

Fish Lake Trail

Sprague Creek

Lincoln Lake Trail

Going-to-the-Sun Road

Lincoln Creek

Hypsometry

10,000
9,000
8,000
7,000
6,000
5,000
4,000
3,000

Elevation (feet)

53 80 000

53 80 000

the differences in the forest understory here compared to that of the far bank. It will take centuries for the forest to recover from the clearing of underbrush and the compacting of soil that once took place here. Follow the paved path back to Going-to-the-Sun Road, then turn right (north) to return to your vehicle.

Key Points

0.0 Trail of the Cedars Trailhead. Follow the boardwalk.

0.4 Bridge below Avalanche Gorge. Follow paved trail down south bank of stream.

0.7 Old Avalanche Creek Campground entrance on Going-to-the-Sun Road.

6 Avalanche Lake

Type of hike: Out-and-back
Total distance: 4.6 miles (7.4 km) round-trip to foot of lake

Time required: 2 to 4 hours
Elevation change: 505-foot gain

Finding the trailhead: Trail of the Cedars Trailhead, across from Avalanche Picnic Area on Going-to-the-Sun Road.

The Hike

The Avalanche Lake Trail is one of the most popular hikes in Glacier, due to its gentle grade and spectacular destination. Hikers seeking solitude should go elsewhere, since throngs of bear bell–bedecked tourists are a given at the height of the season.

Avalanche Lake

RF 1:177,500

Kilometers 0 — 4

Miles 0 — 4

N

Lake Evangeline

McDonald Creek

The Loop

The Salamander Glacier

Garden Wall

Camas Lake

Haystack Butte

Weeping Wall

Camas Creek Trail

5400000

Arrow Lake

Heavens Peak
8987ft
2739m

Triple Arches

Mount Oberlin
8180ft
2493m

Mount Clements
8760 ft
2670 m

Logan Pass

Mount Vaught
8850ft
2697m

Trail of the Cedars

6

Avalanche Creek

Avalanche Creek Trail

Hidden Lake

Stanton Mountain
7750ft
2362m

Avalanche Creek

Avalanche Lake

Continental Divide

Lake McDonald

Mount Brown
8565 ft
2610 m

5390000 McDonald Falls

Johns Lake

Mt. Brown Lookout Tr.

Snyder Lakes

Sperry Glacier

5390

Lake McDonald

Snyder Lake Trail

Sperry Chalet

Gunsight Mountain
9258 ft
2821 m

Sprague Creek

Fish Lake

Sprague Creek

Going-to-the-Sun Road

Fish Lake Trail

Lincoln Lake Trail

Creek

Lincoln

5380000

5380000

Hypsometry

Elevation (feet)
10,000
9,000
8,000
7,000
6,000
5,000
4,000
3,000

Elevation (feet)

The hike begins on the Trail of the Cedars, a wheelchair-accessible boardwalk that winds between boles of huge cedars and cottonwoods to Avalanche Gorge. The gorge was formed by the force of a stream cutting down through argillite beds, creating fantastic bowls and chutes in the rock. The spray from small waterfalls provides the moisture needed to sustain the profusion of mosses that drape the rocks surrounding the gorge. Water ouzels fly along the watercourse, occasionally diving into the churning water, emerging unharmed to execute "pushups" on the rocks along the stream.

The Avalanche Lake Trail follows the west rim of the gorge through stands of western hemlock, identified by its drooping topmost leader. This tree is limited to areas of high rainfall. The trail winds upward through the forest, following the course of Avalanche Creek. Across the valley to the northeast, the Hidden Creek Valley joins the valley of Avalanche Creek. The trail continues upward through sparse timber and dense underbrush until it reaches the foot of the lake.

Avalanche Lake is rimmed by steep cliffs on three sides. Bearhat Mountain forms the east wall of the valley, while the west wall is formed by Mount Brown. To the south, at the head of the valley, numerous waterfalls cascade downward from the hanging cirque formed by Sperry Glacier, which cannot be seen from the lake.

Key Points

0.0 Trail of the Cedars boardwalk.

0.3 Trail leaves boardwalk and crosses Avalanche Creek. Junction with Avalanche Creek Trail. Turn left.

2.3 Foot of Avalanche Lake. (**Option:** Continue 0.8 mile to the head of Avalanche Lake.)

4.6 Return to trailhead.

Logan Pass and the St. Mary Valley

Logan Pass is one of the most popular destinations in Glacier National Park. High above the timberline at 6,646 feet, it sits in a landscape of vast alpine meadows dotted with bulb-shaped blossoms of beargrass as well as other wildflowers. Stark crags rise all around, and mountain goats are often spotted on the grassy swards below the cliffs. The visitor center at Logan Pass has limited parking, and during the height of summer, visitors should come early or plan to take the shuttle.

The St. Mary River drainage is bisected by the Going-to-the-Sun Road, which provides easy access to a well-developed trail system. The most dominant feature of the area is St. Mary Lake itself, reflecting stunning vistas of the surrounding mountains. The front ranges are formed of Grinnell argillite, which imparts a characteristic reddish tint to the peaks. The rain shadow formed by the Continental Divide and the dry winds that scour this area explains the lack of snow on the eastern peaks during July and August. The peaks along the backbone of the divide have snowfields that linger year-round. A few small glaciers remain in the higher cirques, harking back to the time when the entire park was buried in ice.

The grassy flats around Rising Sun provide important winter range for elk, and in autumn the bugling of bulls echoes from the valley walls. The valley is dominated by lodgepole pines at its lower elevations, with a few stands of aspen in areas of waterlogged soil. Higher up, spruce and subalpine fir are interspersed with beargrass and other wildflowers. Dry south-facing slopes are covered with the drought-resistant grasses that dominate the high plains to the east.

The town of St. Mary provides visitor facilities, including a first-rate lodge that occasionally serves lake whitefish, a delicacy caught in nearby lakes. A visitor center just inside the park boundary gives out information and backcountry permits. Half a mile beyond the entrance station is the St. Mary auto campground. Rising Sun includes a motel and camp store, as well as a park-run auto campground. A commercial boat runs tours from Rising Sun, featuring scenic and interpretive loop cruises on St. Mary Lake.

7 Hidden Lake

Type of hike: Out-and-back
Total distance: 3 miles (4.8 km) round-trip to overlook; 6 miles (9.7 km) round-trip to lake

Time required: 1.5 to 2.5 hours to overlook; 3 to 5 hours to lake
Elevation change: 550-foot gain, 675-foot loss

Finding the trailhead: Trail begins immediately behind Logan Pass Visitor Center.

The Hike

The trail to Hidden Lake provides some of the quickest access to high alpine country in Glacier National Park. It starts as a boardwalk, climbing moderately through fields of wildflowers above the Logan Pass Visitor Center. It tops out at Hidden Lake Pass in the shadow of Clements Mountain. From the pass, Reynolds Mountain dominates the southern skyline, while Bearhat Mountain rises on the far side of islet-strewn Hidden Lake. About 0.3 mile farther is an overlook point, from which the trail descends almost 700 feet to the north shore of the lake. Hidden Lake is reputed to contain large but wary cutthroat trout, which offer challenging angling.

Key Points

- **0.0** Trail sign behind Logan Pass Visitor Center.
- **1.4** Hidden Lake Pass.
- **1.5** Hidden Lake Overlook. Trail descends fairly steeply to Hidden Lake.
- **3.0** Hidden Lake.
- **6.0** Return to trailhead.

Hidden Lake

RF 1:177,500

Kilometers 0 — 4

Miles 0 — 4

N

Many Glacier

Iceberg Lake

North Swiftcurrent Glacier

Redrock Falls

Bullhead Lake

Swiftcurrent Lake

Road Closed Winter

Swiftcurrent Pass

Swiftcurrent Glacier

Lake Josephine

Grinnell Lake

Granite Park Chalet

The Loop

The Salamander Glacier

Grinnell Glacier

Mount Gould
9553 ft
2911 m

Canyon Creek

Cracker Lake

Siyeh Glacier

Mount Siyeh
10014 ft
3052 m

Highline Trail

Garden Wall

Haystack Butte

Weeping Wall

Piegan Pass

Triple Arches

Mount Oberlin
8180 ft
2493 m

Going - to - the - Sun Road

Piegan Glacier

Sexton Glacier

Mount Clements
8760 ft
2670 m

Siyeh Bend

Going-to-the-Sun Mountain
9642 ft
2939 m

Logan Pass

7

Reynolds Mountain
9125 ft
2781 m

Jackson Glacier Overlook

Hidden Lake

Reynolds Creek

Avalanche Creek

Avalanche Lake

Continental Divide

Florence Falls

Hypsometry

Elevation (feet)
10,000
9,000
8,000
7,000
6,000
5,000
4,000
3,000

Mount Brown
8565 ft
2610 m

Snyder Lakes

Sperry Glacier

Gunsight Mountain
9258 ft
2821 m

Sperry Chalet

Mount Jackson
10052 ft
3064 m

Jackson Glacier

Mount Logan
9289 ft
2816 m

Blackfoot Glacier

Lake Ellen Wilson

8 Haystack Butte

Type of hike: Out-and-back
Total distance: 6.8 miles (10.9 km) round-trip

Time required: 3 to 6 hours
Elevation change: 600-foot gain, 200-foot loss

Finding the trailhead: The trail begins at Logan Pass, across the highway from the visitor center.

The Hike

This section of the Highline Trail is one of the most popular hikes in the park, owing to its spectacular vistas, excellent wildlife-viewing opportunities, and low level of difficulty. The trail follows the west face of the Continental Divide, maintaining a relatively constant elevation. The Highline Trail crosses excellent habitat for many types of wildlife, and the open subalpine meadows of the Garden Wall allow easy viewing of wild creatures in their natural environments. Columbia ground squirrels abound in the alpine tundra, and hoary marmots and pikas live among the boulders of talus slopes. Look for mountain goats and bighorn sheep near the bases of the cliffs and among stands of fir. Raptors often soar on thermals high above the alpine meadows, hunting for rodents. Please do not feed the wildlife, in the interest of keeping it wild.

The trail begins at Logan Pass, winding through twisted forms of subalpine firs and Engelmann spruce. Strong winter winds blow ice particles that tear the branches from the windward side of the trees, giving them a flaglike appearance. In areas of especially high wind, all exposed branches may be pruned by windblown ice, creating a low, matlike growth form called krummholz in adult spruce and firs. Watch for mountain goats here.

After several hundred yards, the trail winds around a sheer cliff face, high above the valley below. There is a cable handrail for nervous travelers. The trail then continues northward through open stands of fir, following in the shadow of the Garden Wall. This landform was created by the action of glaciers moving down valleys on both sides of a mountain mass. The resulting knife-edge ridge is called an arête. Winter avalanches hurtle down from its heights on a regular basis, clearing broad swaths in the trees and shrubs. Across the valley, Mounts Oberlin, Clements, and Cannon cradle a high-hanging basin, formed by glaciers, from which Bird Woman Falls cascades almost 500 feet to the valley floor.

The path soon levels off for a long stretch, proceeding northward beneath the towering cliffs. Views now expand to include Heavens Peak to the northwest, and soon there are views of the rest of the Livingston Range stretching away into Canada. The trail ultimately emerges into an open bowl clad in tundra. Beargrass and other wildflowers bloom here beside slender rills and stairstep cascades. The trail climbs gently to the pass behind Haystack Butte, a rounded promontory that juts into the Logan Creek Valley. Golden-mantled ground squirrels, identified by the alternating stripes of black and blond on their backs, inhabit the slopes around Haystack Butte. From here there are fine views southward to Logan Pass, with Reynolds Mountain presiding over it and a slender skein of water descending into the valley below. This is the turnaround point, and it makes an ideal lunch spot. Huge boulders have fallen into the saddle from the cliffs above; rest on a rock to avoid damaging the fragile vegetation.

Haystack Butte

RF 1:177,500

Kilometers 0 — 4

Miles 0 — 4

N

Many Glacier

Iceberg Lake

Redrock Falls

North Swiftcurrent Glacier

Road Closed in Winter

Swiftcurrent Lake

Bullhead Lake

Swiftcurrent Pass

Swiftcurrent Glacier

Lake Josephine

Grinnell Lake

Granite Park Chalet

The Loop

The Salamander Glacier

Grinnell Glacier

Mount Gould 9553 ft 2911 m

Canyon Creek

Cracker Lake

Siyeh Glacier

Haystack Butte

Weeping Wall

Triple Arches

Garden Wall

Highline Trail

Piegan Pass

Mount Oberlin 8180 ft 2493 m

Piegan Glacier

Sexton Glacier

Mount Clements 8760 ft 2670 m

Logan Pass

Siyeh Bend

8

Going-to-the-Sun Road

Hidden Lake

Reynolds Mountain 9125 ft 2781 m

Jackson Glacier Overlook

Avalanche Creek

Avalanche Lake

Continental Divide

Reynolds Creek

Florence Falls

Mount Brown 8565 ft 2610 m

Hypsometry

Snyder Lakes

Sperry Glacier

Gunsight Mountain 9258 ft 2821 m

10,000
9,000
8,000
7,000
6,000
5,000
4,000
3,000

Sperry Chalet

Mount Jackson 10052 ft 3064 m

Jackson Glacier

Elevation (feet)

Lake Ellen Wilson

Blackfoot Glacier

Mount Logan 9239 ft 2816 m

Key Points

0.0 Logan Pass.
3.4 Saddle behind Haystack Butte.
6.8 Return to trailhead.

8/26/13

St. Mary and Virginia Falls

Type of hike: Out-and-back
Total distance: 2.4 miles (3.9 km) round-trip to St. Mary Falls; 3.6 miles (5.8 km) round-trip to Virginia Falls

Time required: 1.5 to 3.5 hours, depending on destination
Elevation change: 285-foot gain, 260-foot loss

Finding the trailhead: The trailhead is located on the Going-to-the-Sun Road, about 0.3 mile west of Baring Creek.

The Hike

This trail is a short and pleasant stroll through sun–dappled forest to several roaring waterfalls in the valley below Going-to-the-Sun Road. From the trailhead, the trail descends to the valley floor, past well-marked trail junctions, to cross the river immediately below the thundering cataract of St. Mary Falls. Beyond the falls the forest opens up, affording views of Little Chief and Dusty Star Mountains. The path winds around the ends of several hillocks to reach Virginia Creek, which it follows for 0.5 mile past a narrow gorge. The hike ends at equally impressive Virginia Falls, which emerges from the mouth of a hanging valley. A short spur on the right leads you to the foot of the falls.

St. Mary and Virginia Falls

RF 1:177,500

Hypsometry	
	10,000
	9,000
	8,000
	7,000
	6,000
	5,000
	4,000
	3,000
Elevation (feet)	

Key Points

0.0 Trail sign. Trail descends toward the St. Mary River.

0.3 Junction with the Piegan Pass Trail. Turn right for St. Mary Falls and Virginia Falls.

0.7 Junction with St. Mary Trail. Turn left for falls.

1.2 Trail crosses St. Mary River at St. Mary Falls. Trail continues, ascending the south side of the St. Mary Valley.

1.8 Virginia Falls.

3.6 Return to trailhead.

1O Sun Point Nature Trail

Type of hike: Out-and-back
Total distance: 1.3 miles (2.1 km) round-trip

Time required: 45 minutes to 1.5 hours
Elevation change: Minimal

Finding the trailhead: The trail begins from the Sun Point parking area, 11 miles east of Logan Pass on Going-to-the-Sun Road.

The Hike

This short trek offers excellent views of St. Mary Lake and concludes with a stunning waterfall. It is a self-guiding nature trail with pamphlets available at the beginning of the trail.

The hike begins by dipping to reach a fork in the trail. Bear left on a spur path to make the short climb to Sun Point, which overlooks St. Mary Lake. A sign points out the names of the massive summits that ring the lake. These summits have a reddish cast because they are composed of Grinnell argillite,

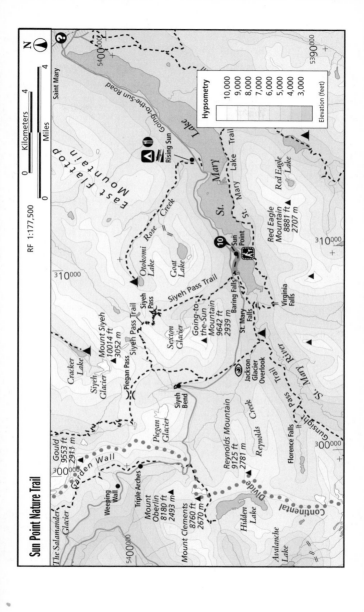

Sun Point Nature Trail

RF 1:177,500

N

0   4   Kilometers
0   4   Miles

Hypsometry

10,000
9,000
8,000
7,000
6,000
5,000
4,000
3,000

Elevation (feet)

The Salamander Glacier

Gould
9553 ft
2911 m

Garden Wall

Weeping Wall

Triple Arches

Cracker Lake

Mount Oberlin
8180 ft
2493 m

Mount Siyeh
10014 ft
3052 m

Siyeh Glacier

Piegan Pass

Piegan Glacier

Siyeh Bend

Siyeh Pass

Siyeh Pass Trail

Siyeh Pass Trail

East Flattop Mountain

Rose Creek

Otokomi Lake

Goat Lake

Rising Sun

Saint Mary

Going-to-the-Sun Road

St. Mary Lake

St. Mary Lake Trail

Sun Point

Baring Falls

Sexton Glacier

Going-to-the-Sun Mountain
9642 ft
2939 m

Mount Clements
8760 ft
2670 m

Reynolds Mountain
9125 ft
2781 m

Hidden Lake

Avalanche Lake

Continental Divide

Reynolds Creek

Florence Falls

Jackson Glacier Overlook

St. Mary Falls

Virginia Falls

St. Mary River

Gunsight Pass Trail

Red Eagle Mountain
8881 ft
2707 m

Red Eagle Lake

a mudstone that is rich in iron and turns red as the iron oxi-dizes. During the uplift that created the Rocky Mountains some sixty-five million years ago, these old seafloor sedi-ments were tilted skyward, and the direction of the tilt can be seen today in the slant of the rock strata.

Return to the main trail and hike westward as it runs level above the shores of St. Mary Lake. A sparse growth of wind-torn lodgepole pines allows fine views of the water and the peaks that surround it. The turquoise glacier-fed lake is almost 300 feet deep, occupying a basin that was carved out by a massive valley glacier during the Pleistocene epoch. The ice was so deep that it reached the tops of the highest summits. The U-shaped cross-section of the valley is the tell-tale footprint of the long-vanished glacier. As the path crosses sliderock beneath a low cliff, note the green bedrock. This is Appekuny argillite, older than the Grinnell formation but made of a similar mudstone.

The path enters a woodland of spruce and Douglas fir as it approaches Baring Creek. Bear left at the junction as the main trail crosses a footlog to reach the base of Baring Falls. This impressive cascade drops across a sheer cliff of argillite into a natural amphitheater in the rock. Turn around here and retrace your steps to complete the hike.

11 Beaver Pond Trail

Type of hike: Loop
Total distance: 3.4 miles
(5.5 km)

Time required: 1.5 to 3 hours
Elevation change: 120-foot gain

Finding the trailhead: Take Going-to-the-Sun Road 0.25 mile east from St. Mary to a paved road entering on the south before the park entrance station. Take this road, bearing right, about 0.5 mile to a parking lot with a trailhead sign. Hike up to the old St. Mary Ranger Station to begin the loop.

The Hike

Though lacking in spectacular scenery, this hike runs through a pleasant landscape of coniferous forests, grassy meadows, and aspen groves. It receives few visitors and is thus a good place to find solitude.

The trail begins by climbing the hill to the original St. Mary Ranger Station, built in 1910 of native timber. Behind the old buildings, the path ascends to a low ridgetop that bears the scars of periodic lightning fires. This ridge is a terminal moraine of the glacier that carved the St. Mary Valley, bulldozed into place at the toe of the glacier by the slow but inexorable surge of glacial ice. The path follows the ridgetop through shady stands of Douglas fir and grassy meadows, providing views of Red Eagle Mountain to the southwest and East Flattop Mountain to the north. Eventually the woodland opens onto rank grasslands bordered by aspen groves, and Split Mountain appears up the Red Eagle Creek Valley.

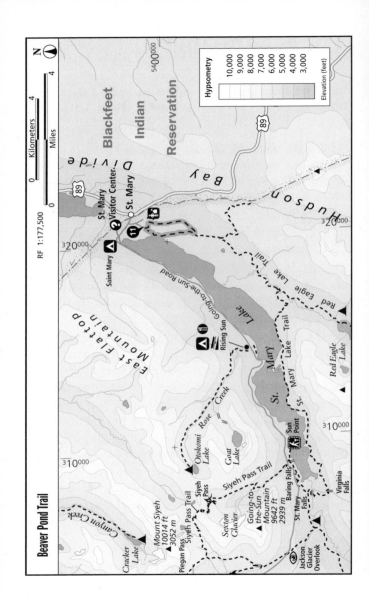

Beaver Pond Trail

RF 1:177,500

N

Hypsometry

10,000
9,000
8,000
7,000
6,000
5,000
4,000
3,000

Elevation (feet)

Kilometers   0   4
Miles   0   4

Blackfeet

Indian

Reservation

St. Mary Divide

St. Mary
Visitor Center

St. Mary

Bay

Hudson

89

Saint Mary

Red Eagle Lake Trail

Going-to-the-Sun Road

East Flattop Mountain

Rising Sun

St. Mary Lake

St. Mary Lake Trail

Red Eagle Lake

Sun Point

Canyon Creek

Cracker Lake

Mount Siyeh
10014 ft
3052 m

Piegan Pass

Siyeh Pass Trail

Siyeh Pass

Rose Creek

Otokomi Lake

Goat Lake

Siyeh Pass Trail

Sexton Glacier

Going-to-the-Sun Mountain
9642 ft
2939 m

Baring Falls

St. Mary Falls

Virginia Falls

Jackson Glacier Overlook

89

The trail soon reaches a stagnant pond dammed by beavers. The beavers are long gone, but their pond is a good spot to look for birdlife. The trail then turns west and descends to abandoned Red Eagle Road, now a hiking trail. Turn right as the old road parallels the shore of St. Mary Lake, yielding occasional views of the water. The roadbed bears travelers back to the parking lot to complete the loop.

Key Points

0.1   Old St. Mary Ranger Station. Trail departs behind the buildings.

1.3   Beaver pond.

1.8   Junction with Red Eagle Trail. Turn right onto old road.

3.4   Old roadbed returns to trailhead.

Two Medicine Valley

The mountains that form this part of the Continental Divide were known to the Blackfeet Indians as the "Backbone of the World." They used the Two Medicine area for vision quests as well as hunting and gathering. The towering spires and sheer cliffs still provoke awe in travelers searching for a haven from the hurried pace of the modern world. A well-worn network of trails here provides access to a landscape of unequaled beauty, visiting peaceful lakes and dizzying heights.

In this eastern part of the park, sheer mountains rise abruptly from the rolling Great Plains, providing a mixture of flora and fauna from widely different biotic communities. The alpine communities of higher elevations grade into grasslands adapted to the more arid plains. Since the mountains of the divide form a barrier to moisture-laden maritime air masses, this area occupies a rain shadow. Precipitation on the plains falls mostly in summer in the form of brief thunderstorms, following the rainfall regime of the high plains. This pattern of precipitation favors shallow-rooted grasses over larger trees and shrubs, thus accounting for the lack of lush forests on this side of the divide.

Area wildlife reflects the drier vegetation. Bighorn sheep, favoring grasses as forage, are seen more commonly in this drier area than are mountain goats. Golden eagles soar on updrafts created by the warmth of the sun on open grasslands. Waterfalls block the immigration of native fish into most of the high lakes; fish found in most of these lakes were introduced at some time in the past. These planted fish have successfully made a place for themselves in the lake ecosystems and now sustain their populations naturally, without supplementary plantings by the National Park Service.

Dry winds roar through the high mountain passes here, a dominant force in shaping the patterns of vegetation in the Front Range. These same winds reach speeds upwards of 80 miles per hour and cause incredibly high wind-chill factors in winter.

12 Running Eagle Falls

Type of hike: Out-and-back
Total distance: 0.6 mile (1 km) round-trip

Time required: 15 to 45 minutes
Elevation change: Minimal

Finding the trailhead: The trail begins at the Red Eagle Falls parking area, on the north side of Two Medicine Road about 2 miles past the park entrance station.

The Hike

This short stroll leads to an odd waterfall that emerges from an underground cave during late summer but pours over a higher sill during spring runoff. There are plans in the works to pave the trail and make it accessible to wheelchairs as far as the banks of Two Medicine Creek. A wheelchair-accessible section leads visitors to a view point of the falls just short of Dry Fork Creek and returns via a pleasant path along the Two Medicine River, forming a short loop.

The walk begins in an open woodland of spruce and fir underlain by a vigorous growth of shrubs. A few old cottonwoods date from floods in years past. Cottonwood seedlings require bare soil and plenty of groundwater to get established, a combination that is unique to rivers that scour their banks with periodic floods. The two major peaks that are visible along the way are Rising Wolf Mountain to the northwest and Spot Mountain to the northeast. The path soon reaches a broad stretch of bare gravel where the Dry Fork joins the Two Medicine River. The Dry Fork floods each spring during snowmelt season, and the force

Running Eagle Falls

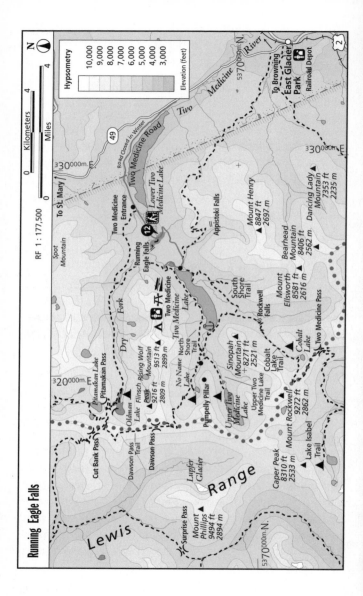

RF 1 : 177,500

Hypsometry

Elevation (feet)
10,000
9,000
8,000
7,000
6,000
5,000
4,000
3,000

Lewis

Range

Surprise Pass

Mount Phillips
9494 ft
2894 m

Cut Bank Pass

Dawson Pass Trail

Pitamakan Lake

Pitamakan Pass

Oldman Lake

Flinsch Peak
9216 ft
2809 m

Rising Wolf Mountain
9513 ft
2899 m

Dawson Pass

Lupfer Glacier

Caper Peak
8310 ft
2533 m

Lake Isabel Trail

Mount Rockwell
9272 ft
2862 m

Pumpelly Pillar

Upper Two Medicine Lake

Upper Two Medicine Lake Trail

No Name Lake

North Shore Trail

Sinopah Mountain
8271 ft
2521 m

Cobalt Lake

Cobalt Lake Trail

Two Medicine Pass

Mount Ellsworth
8581 ft
2616 m

Rockwell Falls

South Shore Trail

Two Medicine Lake

Two Medicine

Running Eagle Falls

Appistoki Falls

Mount Henry
8847 ft
2697 m

Bearhead Mountain
8406 ft
2562 m

Dancing Lady Mountain
7353 ft
2235 m

Spot Mountain

Dry Fork

To St. Mary

Two Medicine Entrance

Lower Two Medicine Lake

Two Medicine Road

Road Closed in Winter

49

Two Medicine River

To Browning

East Glacier Park

Railroad Depot

2

330 000m. E.

330 000m. E.

5370 000m. N.

5370 000m. N.

320 000m. E.

N

0 1 2 3 4 Kilometers

0 1 2 3 4 Miles

of these periodic deluges is sufficient to sweep the banks bare of vegetation.

After crossing a footbridge over the river, the path climbs to an overlook below Running Eagle Falls. This unique cataract pours over a sill of stone 40 feet high during early summer. But when the river level drops, the upper channel dries up and the falls emerge from a hidden grotto some 20 feet below the upper lip. This odd phenomenon led early visitors to nickname the site "Trick Falls." A rough and uneven path closes the remaining distance to the foot of the falls, which thunder into a placid pool of deep turquoise water.

13 Appistoki Falls

Type of hike: Out-and-back
Total distance: 1.2 miles (1.9 km) round-trip

Time required: 30 to 60 minutes
Elevation change: 320-foot gain

Finding the trailhead: Trail departs from the marked Scenic Point Trailhead on Two Medicine Road, about 4 miles beyond the park entrance station.

The Hike

This trail climbs to a small waterfall in the barren gorge of Appistoki Creek. It begins in a pleasant woodland of sub-alpine fir, lit by the blossoms of beargrass in early summer of favorable years. Beargrass is not a grass at all but a member of the lily family, with great bulb-shaped clusters of tiny white flowers. It blooms on a three-year cycle, with most

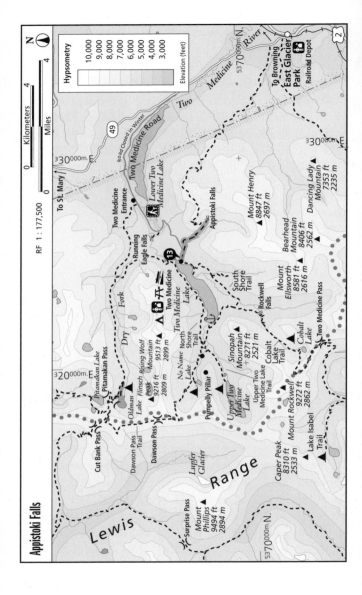

Appistoki Falls

RF 1 : 177,500

Hypsometry

Elevation (feet)

- 10,000
- 9,000
- 8,000
- 7,000
- 6,000
- 5,000
- 4,000
- 3,000

N

Kilometers

0   4

Miles

0   4

To St Mary

Two Medicine Road

Road Closed in Winter

49

Two Medicine River

5370000m. N.

330000m. E.

To Browning

East Glacier Park

Railroad Depot

2

Lower Two Medicine Lake

Two Medicine Entrance

Running Eagle Falls

Dry Fork

Appistoki Falls

Mount Henry
8847 ft
2697 m

Dancing Lady Mountain
7353 ft
2235 m

330000m. E.

Two Medicine Lake

13

South Shore Trail

Rockwell Falls

Bearhead Mountain
8406 ft
2562 m

Mount Ellsworth
8581 ft
2616 m

Cobalt Lake

Two Medicine Pass

North Shore Trail

No Name Lake

Two Medicine Lake

Sinopah Mountain
8271 ft
2521 m

Cobalt Lake Trail

Pitamakan Lake

Pitamakan Pass

320000m. E.

Oldman Lake

Flinsch Peak
9216 ft
2809 m

Rising Wolf Mountain
9513 ft
2899 m

Pumpelly Pillar

Upper Two Medicine Lake

Upper Two Medicine Lake Trail

Cut Bank Pass

Dawson Pass Trail

Dawson Pass

Lupfer Glacier

Mount Rockwell
9272 ft
2862 m

Caper Peak
8310 ft
2533 m

Lake Isabel Trail

Surprise Pass

Mount Phillips
9494 ft
2894 m

Lewis

Range

5370000m. N.

plants in a given locale coming into bloom during the same year. The path rises gently through the forest, which thins with increasing elevation. The barren face of Appistoki Peak looms to the west, while the similar summit of Scenic Point rises to the east.

The trail strikes Appistoki Creek at the base of the mountains as it emerges from a desolate vale between the peaks. Turn right at the junction to reach an overlook on the rim of a rocky ravine. From here, the main waterfall can be seen as it slides down across an inclined face of stone, with pools and lesser cascades below it.

14 Two Medicine Lake

Type of hike: Loop
Total distance: 7.6 miles (11.9 km) with no side trips

Time required: 4 to 7 hours
Elevation change: 340-foot gain and loss

Finding the trailhead: The loop begins at Two Medicine Lake's South Shore Trailhead, at the west end of the Two Medicine lower boat dock parking lot. The hike ends at Two Medicine Campground, about 0.2 mile from boat dock. Boat users may enter the trail system at the lake's upper boat dock.

The Hike

This trail makes a circuit around Two Medicine Lake. It travels inland for most of its length, but offers periodic views of the water and the glacier-carved peaks that surround it. The loop requires a full day of traveling for most folks; if you are less ambitious, you might opt to hike out to Paradise Point

Two Medicine Lake

RF 1 : 177,500

N

Hypsometry

Elevation (feet)

10,000
9,000
8,000
7,000
6,000
5,000
4,000
3,000

0   4
Kilometers

0   4
Miles

Lewis   Range

Surprise Pass

Mount
Phillips
9494 ft
2894 m

Cut Bank Pass

Lupfer
Glacier

Dawson Pass
Trail

Caper Peak
8310 ft
2533 m

Dawson Pass

Pitamakan Lake
Pitamakan Pass

Oldman
Lake

Flinsch
Peak
9216 ft
2809 m

Rising Wolf
Mountain
9513 ft
2899 m

Dry   Fork

Mount Rockwell
9272 ft
2862 m

Lake Isabel
Trail

Pumpelly Pillar

No Name
Lake

North Shore
Trail

Upper Two
Medicine Lake

Upper Two
Medicine Lake
Trail

Sinopah
Mountain
8271 ft
2521 m

Cobalt
Lake Trail

Cobalt
Lake

Running
Eagle Falls

Two Medicine
Lake

Two Medicine

14

South Shore
Trail

Rockwell
Falls

Two Medicine Pass

Mount
Ellsworth
8581 ft
2616 m

To St. Mary

49

Two Medicine Road

Road Closed in Winter

330000m. E.

Two Medicine
Entrance

Lower Two
Medicine Lake

Appistoki Falls

Two   Medicine   River

Mount Henry
8847 ft
2697 m

Bearhead
Mountain
8406 ft
2562 m

Dancing Lady
Mountain
7353 ft
2235 m

To Browning

East Glacier
Park

Railroad Depot

2

320000m. E.

330000m. E.

5370000m. N.

5370000m. N.

for fine views, or take the tour boat to the head of the lake and hike one of the legs of the loop back to your vehicle.

The hike begins with a modest climb into subalpine firs south of Two Medicine Lake. At the top of the rise is an intersection; here, a spur path descends to Paradise Point on the lakeshore. This nice side trip drops through the trees, then crosses rank meadows to reach the tip of the headland. Paradise Point is the tip of an alluvial fan, built up as sediments carried down from the mountains by Paradise Creek poured into the lake and settled out as the water lost its speed. A gravel beach offers outstanding views of the surrounding peaks without the crowds that throng the foot of the lake.

Meanwhile, the main trail wanders inland, passing old beaver ponds and wetlands. Open meadows beside the marshes offer outstanding views of Appistoki Peak and Never Laughs Mountain to the south, Sinopah Mountain above the head of the lake, and Rising Wolf Mountain beyond the far shore. A footbridge leads across Aster Creek, and on the far bank a spur trail spans the short distance to Aster Falls, then climbs steadily to the Aster Park Overlook.

The Two Medicine loop now charts a level westward course through a loose woodland of fir and pine, ultimately crossing a suspension bridge at Paradise Creek. This substantial stream riffles through picturesque channels in the slanted bedrock. On its far bank is a junction; bear right as the path skirts the foot of Sinopah Mountain. As the trail winds around the north face of Sinopah, it crosses avalanche slopes that offer fine views of the lake. Be alert for grizzly bears in this area.

A steady descent leads into the spruce forest at the head of the lake. Here, a short stroll leads down to the boat dock while the loop route leads westward. The spruce trees soon thin out, and Pumpelly Pillar can be seen ahead. After crossing the headwaters of the Two Medicine River, the trail reaches an intersection near Twin Falls. Turn left to visit the falls, a double cascade that descends from the Bighorn Basin, or turn right to complete the loop.

The main trail follows signs for Dawson Pass as it runs eastward with fine views of Pumpelly Pillar and Sinopah Mountain. After linking up with the trail from Dawson Pass, the path ascends southward onto an alluvial fan at the base of Rising Wolf Mountain. From here hikers get superb views of the lake, as well as Appistoki Peak and Never Laughs Mountain beyond it. The trail then glides down into lakeshore forest and doesn't emerge again until it reaches the foot of the lake. Follow the trail around Pray Lake to reach the bridge leading to Two Medicine Campground and the end of the hike. Walk about 0.2 mile through the campground to the boat dock.

Key Points

- **0.0** South Shore Trailhead.
- **0.2** Junction with Paradise Point spur (0.4 mile). Bear left for loop.
- **1.2** Junction with Aster Park Trail. Bear right for loop.
- **2.2** Bridge over Paradise Creek.
- **2.3** Junction with Cobalt Lake Trail. Turn right.
- **3.3** Junction with upper boat dock trail. Turn left.
- **3.9** Junction with Upper Two Medicine Trail. Turn right onto Dawson cutoff trail.
- **4.1** Junction with Dawson Pass Trail. Turn right to complete loop.
- **7.4** Trail crosses bridge below Pray Lake to end at Two Medicine Campground.
- **7.6** Return to boat dock.

15 Aster Park

Type of hike: Out-and-back
Total distance: 3.8 miles (6.1 km) round-trip

Time required: 2 to 4 hours
Elevation change: 440-foot gain

Finding the trailhead: The hike begins at the Two Medicine Lake South Shore Trailhead, located at the west end of the Two Medicine lower boat dock parking lot.

The Hike

This route combines the early reaches of the Two Medicine Loop with a spur trail that visits a pretty waterfall and then climbs to a high overlook above Two Medicine Lake.

The hike begins by climbing gently into subalpine forest south of Two Medicine Lake. At the top of the rise is a trail junction, where a spur path descends to Paradise Point on the lakeshore. The main trail wanders inland, passing stagnant wetlands; open meadows beside the marshes offer outstanding views of Appistoki Peak and Never Laughs Mountain to the south, Sinopah Mountain above the head of the lake, and Rising Wolf Mountain beyond the far shore. A footbridge leads across Aster Creek, and on the far bank is the junction with the Aster Park Trail.

Turn left as this spur trail rises gently through the pines and firs. Soon a side path splits away toward the base of Aster Falls, where Aster Creek sluices down through a cleft in the bedrock, arcing downward in ribbonlike streams. The main trail makes several upward switchbacks, then settles into a steady westward grade through the trees. At the top of a low headwall, hikers will get fine aerial views of

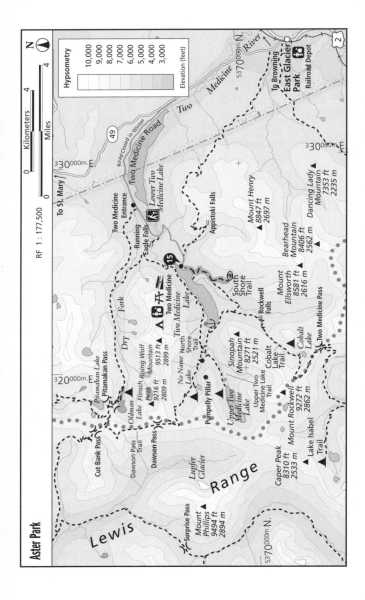

Two Medicine Lake and the surrounding crags. The trail then turns south into the hanging valley of Aster Creek before climbing to its end on a rocky overlook at the edge of the Two Medicine Valley.

Key Points

0.0   South Shore Trailhead.
0.2   Junction with Paradise Point spur (0.4 mile). Bear left for loop.
1.2   Junction with Aster Park Trail. Turn left.
1.3   Spur trail to base of Aster Falls.
1.9   Aster Park Overlook.
3.8   Return to trailhead.

16 Upper Two Medicine Lake

Type of hike: Out-and-back
Total distance: 4.4 miles (7.1 km) round-trip with boat shuttle

Time required: 2 to 3 hours
Elevation change: 440-foot gain

Finding the trailhead: Ferry travelers will begin the hike at the Two Medicine Lake upper boat dock. Hikers intending to walk the whole way will begin at the South Shore Trailhead, located at the west end of the Two Medicine lower boat dock parking lot, and follow the South Shore Trail 3.3 miles to the upper dock.

The Hike

Visitors can combine this spur trail with the Two Medicine Loop for a long day hike of 12.0 miles, or take the tour

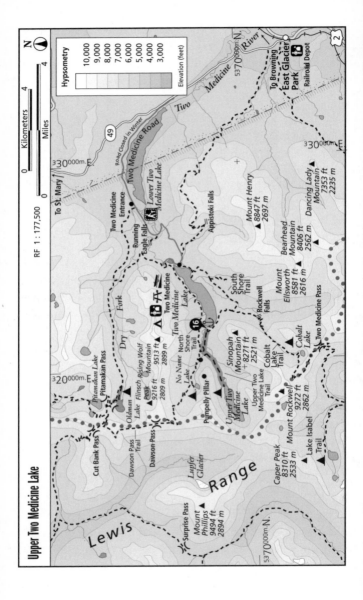

Upper Two Medicine Lake

RF 1 : 177,500

Hypsometry

10,000
9,000
8,000
7,000
6,000
5,000
4,000
3,000

Elevation (feet)

Kilometers
0   4

Miles
0   4

N

To St. Mary

To Browning

East Glacier
Park

Railroad Depot

Two Medicine River

Lower Two
Medicine Lake

Two Medicine Road

Road Closed in Winter

Two Medicine
Entrance

Running
Eagle Falls

Appistoki Falls

Mount Henry
8847 ft
2697 m

Bearhead
Mountain
8406 ft
2562 m

Dancing Lady
Mountain
7353 ft
2235 m

Mount
Ellsworth
8581 ft
2616 m

Rockwell
Falls

South Shore
Trail

Two Medicine
Lake

Two Medicine Pass

Cobalt
Lake

Cobalt
Lake Trail

Sinopah
Mountain
8271 ft
2521 m

North
Shore Trail

No Name
Lake

Two Medicine
Lake

Rising Wolf
Mountain
9513 ft
2899 m

Flinsch
Peak
9216 ft
2809 m

Oldman
Lake

Pitamakan Lake

Pitamakan Pass

Dry Fork

Cut Bank Pass

Dawson Pass
Trail

Dawson Pass

Lupfer
Glacier

Mount
Phillips
9494 ft
2894 m

Surprise Pass

Lewis Range

Caper Peak
8310 ft
2533 m

Mount Rockwell
9272 ft
2862 m

Lake Isabel
Trail

Upper Two
Medicine Lake

Upper Two
Medicine Lake Trail

Pumpelly Pillar

16

330 000m. E

320 000m. E

330 000m. E

5370 000m. N

5370 000m. N

boat to the head of Two Medicine Lake and hike the trail in a couple of hours. If you do take the boat, be sure to find out when scheduled trips depart for the return to the foot of the lake.

From the boat dock, the trail climbs gently through a bottomland forest of spruce. The trees soon thin, and Pumpelly Pillar rises ahead. After crossing the headwaters of the Two Medicine River, the trail reaches an intersection; turn left here for Upper Two Medicine Lake. Just a short distance farther, a spur path leads northward to the base of Twin Falls. These paired cascades descend across a rocky face from their origin in the Bighorn Basin.

Meanwhile, the main trail crosses the creek below the falls and continues its gentle climb up the valley. Where it rises onto the slopes below the cliffs of Pumpelly Pillar, avalanches have cleared away the trees to reveal Mount Rockwell across the valley, as well as the gabled cliffs above the trail. The track soon passes a shallow tarn, then gradually ascends to the foot of Upper Two Medicine Lake. This long, sinuous lake is flanked by glacier-carved walls, and Lone Walker Mountain presides above its head.

Key Points

- **0.0** Two Medicine upper boat dock.
- **0.1** Junction with South Shore Trail. Bear right.
- **0.7** Junction with Dawson cutoff trail. Bear left.
- **0.9** Spur trail to Twin Falls (0.2 mile). Bear left for Upper Two Medicine Lake.
- **2.2** Upper Two Medicine Lake.
- **4.4** Return to boat dock.

Many Glacier

Many Glacier Hotel was built in 1914 by the Great Northern Railway as a destination resort for its rail tourists. The hotel sits among soaring peaks and jagged arêtes that give this area the nickname "America's Little Switzerland." Since the park's creation, myriad trails have been built to reach the scenic wonders surrounding the hotel, making the Many Glacier area a hub for day-hiking activities. Lush meadows and tumbling waterfalls below snowy peaks invite the traveler to pause and contemplate the awe-inspiring beauty of the mountains.

The lower end of the valley is dominated by Lake Sherburne, which was impounded during the early 1920s. The formation of this reservoir inundated the old mining town of Altyn, which had once served as a center for unsuccessful gold and copper operations in the surrounding mountains, as well as an oil boondoggle.

The Many Glacier area is home to many kinds of wildlife. Most prominent is the majestic grizzly bear, frequently seen foraging for bulbs and berries on the open slopes of the surrounding mountains. Mountain goats cavort on the rocky ledges of cliffs, and bighorn sheep ewes with their young sometimes appear in the lowlands around the hotel. The meadows and forests abound with rodents and songbirds of all kinds.

Visitor services are available in the area around the hotel as well as in the nearby town of Babb, on the neighboring Blackfeet Indian Reservation. Trail rides of varying duration depart from the Many Glacier corral above the hotel, and a privately owned tour boat runs between the hotel and the upper end of Lake Josephine, providing interpretive tours and transportation to the upper Cataract Creek drainage. The spacious campground at Many Glacier provides sites for all types of vehicles.

17 Apikuni Falls

Type of hike: Out-and-back
Total distance: 2 miles (3.2 km) round-trip

Time required: 1 to 2 hours
Elevation change: 680-foot gain

Finding the trailhead: Trail begins at the Apikuni Falls Trailhead, 3.3 miles west of the Many Glacier Entrance Station.

The Hike

This short, steep trail leads up to the desolate cliffs of Apikuni Mountain to visit a long and slender waterfall. Hikers will get excellent mountain views throughout the trek.

The hike begins on Apikuni Flats, where grassy meadows offer views of the major peaks up the valley: Mount Gould, with its chiseled countenance; the symmetrical pyramid of Grinnell Point to the north of it; and, between them, the Garden Wall, graced with Salamander and Grinnell Glaciers. At the far edge of the flats, the path undertakes a relentless and calf-burning climb, passing through aspen groves and lodgepole pine stands as it ascends to the base of limestone cliffs. Altyn Peak rises west of Apikuni Creek, while the outer bulwarks of Apikuni Mountain (its reddish summit can be seen through the mouth of the hanging valley above) rise to the east.

The path ultimately climbs onto rocky and barren slopes where only a few firs survive, and the bleached and gnarled skeletons of long-dead whitebark pines rise mournfully to the sky. Swiftcurrent Lake and Lake Josephine can now be

Apikuni Falls

RF 1 : 88,750

Many Glacier Entrance

Many Glacier Road Closed in Winter

Sherburne Lake

Wynn Mountain
8404 ft
2562m

Apikuni
Falls

Cracker Lake Trail

Natinki
Lake

Swiftcurrent
Lake

Falling
Leaf
Lake

Snow
Moon
Lake

Kennedy
Lake

Mount Henkel
8720ft
2658m

Many Glacier

Stump
Lake

South Shore
Lake Josephine
Trail

Iceberg-Ptarmigan Trail

Ptarmigan
Falls

Fishercap
Lake

Swiftcurrent
Lake Trail

Grinnell
Point

North Shore
Lake Josephine
Trail

Lake Josephine

Swiftcurrent Pass Trail

Redrock
Lake

Redrock
Falls

Grinnell Glacier Trail

Grinnell Lake
Trails

Bullhead
Lake

Mount Grinnell
8851 ft
2698m

Hypsometry

10,000
9,000
8,000
7,000
6,000
5,000
4,000
3,000

Elevation (feet)

N

Kilometers

Miles

glimpsed in the valley to the west, while to the south a broad panorama includes Wynn and Allen Mountains arrayed beyond Sherburne Reservoir. Apikuni Falls can be seen ahead, dropping through a cleft in the limestone walls. The path becomes primitive with steep, uneven footing as it navigates a rocky ravine to reach the base of the falls.

18 Swiftcurrent Nature Trail

Type of hike: Loop
Total distance: 2.5 miles (4 km)

Time required: 1 to 2 hours
Elevation change: Minimal

Finding the trailhead: Follow Many Glacier Road past the hotel access road to reach the picnic area at the northwest corner of Swiftcurrent Lake. The trail begins here.

The Hike

This self-guided nature walk makes a circuit around Swiftcurrent Lake. The scenery is spectacular, but hikers will walk past the Many Glacier Hotel and along several roadways, so this is not a wilderness hike. Pamphlets interpreting the landscape are available at the trailhead.

From the picnic area, hike southward as the trail crosses the braided channels of Swiftcurrent Creek. The stream is bordered by a low growth of willows, which thrive in saturated soils. The trail soon enters a lakeshore woodland of subalpine fir and lodgepole pine. Allen Mountain is the prominent peak to the south, with Wynn Mountain to the left of it. After passing the boat dock, the trail crosses Grinnell

Swiftcurrent Nature Trail

RF 1 : 88,750

Hypsometry

Elevation (feet)
10,000
9,000
8,000
7,000
6,000
5,000
4,000
3,000

Kilometers

0   4

Miles

0   4

N

5410⁰⁰⁰

Apikuni Falls

Natinki Lake

Swiftcurrent Lake

Snow Moon Lake

Falling Leaf Lake

South Shore Lake Josephine Trail

Stump Lake

Mount Henkel 8720ft 2658m

Many Glacier

Iceberg-Ptarmigan Trail

Swiftcurrent Pass Trail

Fishercap Lake

Grinnell Point

North Shore Lake Josephine Trail

Lake Josephine

Feather Plume Cutoff Trail

Redrock Lake

Redrock Falls

Grinnell Glacier Trail

Grinnell Lake

Hidden Falls

300⁰⁰⁰

Bullhead Lake

Windmaker Lake

Mount Grinnell 8851ft 2698m

Mount Wilbur 9231ft 2814m

Iceberg Lake

300⁰⁰⁰

North Swiftcurrent Glacier

Swiftcurrent Mountain

Swiftcurrent Glacier

The Salamander Glacier

Swiftcurrent Pass

Granite Park Chalet

5410⁰⁰⁰

Creek and winds onto the south shore of the lake. The massive summit of Altyn Peak now rises to the north. The forest soon thins, and the trail breaks out of it entirely as it reaches Many Glacier Hotel. Spectacular views now encompass Mount Gould to the west, Grinnell Point above the head of the lake, and Mount Wilbur to the northwest. As you follow the lakeshore promenade, scan the lower slopes of Altyn Peak for grizzly bears and bighorn sheep. The trail now runs beside the road, following the lakeshore as it bends westward to return to the picnic area.

Key Points

0.0 Picnic area at northwest corner of Swiftcurrent Lake.

0.8 Upper boat dock.

1.5 Many Glacier Hotel. Follow promenade along lakeshore.

1.9 Junction with Ptarmigan Tunnel Trail. Stay left as loop trail follows lakeshore.

2.5 Trail returns to picnic area.

19 Grinnell Lake

Type of hike: Out-and-back
Total distance: 6.8 miles (10.9 km) round-trip on foot; 1.9 miles (3.1 km) round-trip with boat shuttle

Time required: 3.5 to 7 hours on foot; 1 to 1.5 hours with boat (hiking time only)
Elevation change: 120-foot gain

Finding the trailhead: The trail begins from the southwest corner of the parking lot above Many Glacier Hotel.

The Hike

This trail visits a glacier-fed lake at the base of a stunning waterfall. Grinnell Lake is reached most easily by taking a tour boat across Swiftcurrent Lake and Lake Josephine; hikers who take the tour boat can skip the next two paragraphs. More adventurous hikers can walk through a spectacular mountain landscape past these two lakes to reach the upper boat dock and hook up with the Grinnell Lake Trail. Rangers offer guided interpretive trips to Grinnell Lake via the tour boat on an occasional basis.

From the Many Glacier Hotel parking lot, follow the leg of the Swiftcurrent Nature Trail that crosses the road to the boat dock and then follows the southern shoreline of Swiftcurrent Lake. Subalpine firs form a loose woodland here, and many openings offer views of the surrounding peaks. Grinnell Point is the pyramid-shaped horn that guards the head of the lake, while to the left of it is the grand and bulky edifice of Mount Gould. Farther north, the graceful fin of Mount Wilbur rises above the Swiftcurrent Creek Valley. As the trail approaches the spot where Cataract Creek

Grinnell Lake

RF 1 : 88,750

Hypsometry

| 10,000 |
| 9,000 |
| 8,000 |
| 7,000 |
| 6,000 |
| 5,000 |
| 4,000 |
| 3,000 |

Elevation (feet)

N

Kilometers

Miles

Mount Henkel
8720ft
2658m

Natinki
Lake

Apikuni
Falls

Iceberg-Ptarmigan Trail

Many Glacier

Swiftcurrent
Lake

Stump
Lake

Falling
Leaf
Lake

Snow
Moon
Lake

South Shore
Lake Josephine Trail

Swiftcurrent
Lake Trail

Fishercap
Lake

Grinnell
Point

North Shore
Lake Josephine
Trail

Lake Josephine

Feather Plume Cutoff Trail

Redrock
Lake

Swiftcurrent Pass Trail

Redrock
Falls

Bullhead
Lake

Grinnell Glacier Trail

Grinnell Lake

Falls

Hidden Falls

Grinnell
Lake

Windmaker
Lake

Mount Grinnell
8851 ft
2698m

The
Salamander
Glacier

Grinnell
Glacier

Mount Wilbur
9231 ft
2814m

Iceberg
Lake

North
Swiftcurrent
Glacier

Swiftcurrent
Mountain

Swiftcurrent
Pass

Granite
Park
Chalet

pours into the head of the lake, watch for the bulky massif of Altyn Peak to the northeast.

The path crosses a bridge over Grinnell Creek to reach the Upper Swiftcurrent Boat Dock; turn left here for the short and modest climb through the trees that leads to the foot of Lake Josephine. The route now leads along the north shore of this long turquoise lake. Frequent avalanches from the slopes of Grinnell Point have cleared away the trees, leaving a lush growth of herbaceous plants. Superb views from the lakeshore are dominated by Mount Gould, with the much smaller summit of Angel Wing Mountain projecting from its west face like a flying buttress. Allen Mountain rises beyond the opposite shore, draped with slender waterfalls during early summer. After passing a junction with the Grinnell Glacier Trail, the main trail runs through a stand of spruce and then swings south to cross the marshy flats above the head of the lake.

At the southwestern corner of the lake, the path is joined by the trail from the boat dock; tour boat travelers begin the hike here. Turn right as the trail runs westward through the deep shade of a spruce woodland that is sheltered from winter gales by the surrounding ridges. The path ultimately makes a final crossing of Grinnell Creek to reach the shores of Grinnell Lake. The luminous aquamarine color of the water is derived from glacial flour, a finely pulverized rock sediment suspended in the lake. As sunlight enters the water, it is diffracted by the suspended silt so that only light in the blue and green parts of the spectrum can escape.

The lake occupies a natural amphitheater at the foot of Angel Wing. On the opposite shore, Grinnell Falls drops 1,000 feet across sheer cliffs, bringing meltwater from Grinnell Glacier into the lake. The pile of gravel above the head of the falls is a terminal moraine pushed into place by a surge of this glacier that took place in the late 1880s. Grinnell Glacier cannot be seen from this spot; the snowfield you see at the base of the peak above the falls is actually the tail of the Salamander Glacier.

Key Points

0.0   Many Glacier Hotel parking lot.

0.2   Trail crosses access road to boat dock.

0.6   Trail crosses Grinnell Creek.

0.7   Upper boat dock on Swiftcurrent Lake. Turn left, following signs for Lake Josephine.

0.8   Trail reaches south shore of Lake Josephine. Bear right.

1.8   Junction with Grinnell Glacier Trail. Stay left.

2.2   Junction with Grinnell Glacier cutoff. Bear left to cross Grinnell Creek.

2.5   Junction with boat dock trail. Turn right. Tour boat users start hike here.

3.4   Grinnell Lake.

6.8   Return to trailhead.

20 Iceberg Lake

Type of hike: Out-and-back
Total distance: 9.0 miles (14.6 km) round-trip

Time required: 5 to 8 hours
Elevation change: 1,194-foot gain

Finding the trailhead: The trail departs from the Iceberg-Ptarmigan Trailhead, at the north end of the Swiftcurrent Motor Inn complex, among the cabins behind the coffee shop. A parking pullout there is marked with a trailhead sign.

The Hike

Iceberg Lake is a striking aquamarine tarn surrounded on three sides by towering cliffs. Ice-out may not occur here until mid-July, and the bergs for which the lake was named may be seen floating about well after that date. This stunning destination plus the brilliant wildflowers along the route make the Iceberg Lake Trail one of the most popular hikes in the park. It crosses fine grizzly bear habitat, and bears are seen frequently on the open slopes on both sides of the trail.

The hike begins as a short connecting trail that climbs briskly for several hundred yards to join the main trail coming in from the hotel. The trail then turns northwest, climbing gently along the open slopes high above Wilbur Creek. Look for the magenta spikes of fireweed and the bulblike inflorescences of beargrass (a member of the lily family) early in the season. The trail passes below Altyn Peak, a greenish massif of Appekuny argillite. Mount Wilbur, known to the Blackfeet people as "Heavy Shield Mountain," rises across the valley to the south. The trail passes into open

Iceberg Lake

RF 1 : 88,750

Hypsometry

	Elevation (feet)
	10,000
	9,000
	8,000
	7,000
	6,000
	5,000
	4,000
	3,000

Apikuni Falls

Swiftcurrent Lake

Falling Leaf Lake

Stump Lake

Natinki Lake

Kennedy Lake

Mount Henkel
8720ft
2658m

20 Many Glacier

Iceberg-Ptarmigan Trail

Fishercap Lake

Swiftcurrent Lake Trail

Grinnell Point

Lake Josephine

North Shore Lake Josephine Trail

Redrock Lake

Ptarmigan Falls

Swiftcurrent Pass Trail

Redrock Falls

Bullhead Lake

Mount Wilbur
9231 ft
2814m

Windmaker Lake

Iceberg Lake

North Swiftcurrent Glacier

Swiftcurrent Mountain

Mount Grinnell
8851 ft
2698m

Swiftcurrent Pass

Kilometers
Miles

forests on its way to Ptarmigan Falls, a popular rest stop on hot summer days.

Shortly after passing the falls, the trail reaches the junction with the Ptarmigan Tunnel Trail, then turns southwest along the Ptarmigan Wall through increasingly alpine scenery toward the head of the valley. Looking south, hikers can glimpse a waterfall on Iceberg Creek through the trees. The trail climbs gently as it curls south into the glacial cirque that holds Iceberg Lake.

The 3,000-foot cliffs surrounding the lake provide prime escape habitat for mountain goats, which frequent this area. Talus slopes along the lake's south shore are home to a variety of small mammals, including pikas and ground squirrels. The permanent snowfields at the head of the lake are remnants of a glacier that until recently occupied this basin beneath the cool shadows of Iceberg Peak.

Key Points

0.0 Trail sign.

0.1 Junction with Trail 167. Turn left for Iceberg Lake.

2.3 Trail crosses Ptarmigan Creek at Ptarmigan Falls.

2.4 Junction with Ptarmigan Tunnel Trail. Stay left for Iceberg Lake.

4.4 Trail crosses Iceberg Creek below a nameless tarn.

4.5 Iceberg Lake.

9.0 Return to trailhead.

21 Bullhead Lake

Type of hike: Out-and-back
Total distance: 6.6 miles (10.6 km) round-trip

Time required: 3 to 5 hours
Elevation change: 240-foot gain

Finding the trailhead: The trail begins at the west end of the Swiftcurrent Inn coffee shop parking lot.

The Hike

This hike follows the Swiftcurrent Valley past a chain of pretty lakes, visiting Redrock Falls along the way. The trail begins at the Swiftcurrent Motor Inn and winds westward along the valley floor among groves of tall aspen interspersed with lodgepole pine. The cliffs of Grinnell Point rise to the south, and as the trail runs westward, the summit of Grinnell Peak comes into view along the same ridge.

The trail passes north of Fishercap Lake, which can be glimpsed briefly through a few holes in the vegetation. It then climbs gently, crossing a small stream on its way to Redrock Lake. An intense fire cleared this area in 1936. Notice that harsh growing conditions have stunted the pines and aspens around the lake. The trail continues west, passing Redrock Falls above the head of the lake. About 1.3 miles beyond Redrock Lake, the trail reaches Bullhead Lake. A northward glance reveals Mount Wilbur, Iceberg Peak, and the North Swiftcurrent Glacier on the east face of Swiftcurrent Mountain.

Bullhead Lake

RF 1 : 88,750

N

Hypsometry

Elevation (feet)
10,000
9,000
8,000
7,000
6,000
5,000
4,000
3,000

Kilometers

Miles

Mount Henkel
8720ft
2658m

Many Glacier

Natinki
Lake

Apikuni
Falls

Swiftcurrent
Lake

Iceberg-Ptarmigan Trail

Swiftcurrent Pass Trail

Fishercap
Lake

Redrock
Lake

Swiftcurrent
Lake Trail

Grinnell
Point

North Shore
Lake Josephine
Trail

Stump
Lake

South Shore
Lake Josephine
Trail

Falling
Leaf
Lake

Snow
Moon
Lake

Lake Josephine

Feather Plume Cutoff Trail

Grinnell Glacier Trail

Grinnell
Lake

Hidden
Falls

Trails

Redrock
Falls

Bullhead
Lake

Windmaker
Lake

Mount Grinnell
8851 ft
2698m

Swiftcurrent
Glacier

The
Salamander
Glacier

Mount Wilbur
9231 ft
2814m

Iceberg
Lake

North Swiftcurrent Glacier

Swiftcurrent
Mountain

Swiftcurrent
Pass

Granite
Park
Chalet

Key Points

0.0 Trail sign.

0.2 Junction with horse trail. Stay left for Bullhead Lake. Trail follows floor of Swiftcurrent Valley, climbing gently.

2.0 Redrock Lake.

2.3 Redrock Falls.

3.3 Bullhead Lake.

6.6 Return to trailhead.

For a relatively small park, Waterton supports a diverse array of plants, wildlife, and landscapes, leading to varied opportunities for hikers. Long before they were protected as an international peace park, these mountains and valleys were frequented by people of the Kootenai and Blackfoot tribes, who hunted bison and gathered wild plants here. The first visitors of European descent to take in these breathtaking landscapes were undoubtedly fur traders and missionaries, who came in the late 1850s. In the late 1800s, the discovery of oil in the Cameron Valley drew speculators to establish a drilling operation, which flourished only a short time and is remembered today at Discovery Well historic site. A portion of the present-day park was protected in 1895 as Waterton Lakes Forest Park and later called Kootenai Lakes Forest Reserve.

Protection of this natural treasure was increased in response to the urgings of conservation-minded local residents such as Frederick Godsal and John "Kootenai" Brown. The park was expanded in 1914, then reduced to its present size in 1921. In 1932 an international accord with the United States established the Waterton-Glacier complex as the world's first international peace park. The ensuing years have seen extensive development, highlighted by a complex network of trails, roads, and campgrounds. However, the land beyond the roads retains its wild character.

Waterton township provides most services found in large towns, including a variety of hotel accommodations, restaurants, and stores. There are automobile campgrounds at the townsite and along the Red Rock Parkway; developed picnic facilities exist along all major roads. Motorized boats are allowed in Upper and Middle Waterton Lakes, and all lakes have facilities for launching unpowered boats. In addition, a water taxi on Upper Waterton Lake provides daily service to Crypt Landing and Goat Haunt Ranger Station across the border.

No registration is required for day trips, but overnight expeditions into the backcountry require a special permit, which can be purchased at the visitor center outside Waterton townsite. Backpackers must stay in established campgrounds, although minimum-impact camping in some remote areas may be allowed by special permit. Fishing in the park requires a special license, available for a small fee at the visitor center.

22 Bears Hump

Type of hike: Out-and-back
Total distance: 1.8 miles (2.9 km) round-trip

Time required: 2 to 3 hours
Elevation change: 750-foot gain

Finding the trailhead: The trail begins behind the ranger station at the edge of Waterton townsite.

The Hike

This trail climbs the mountain slopes to visit a spectacular overlook of Waterton Lake. The hike begins with a steady climb through sparse woodlands of aspen and Douglas fir. Looking uphill, the twisted strata of Mount Crandall can be viewed through the trees. This mountain was originally known as Bear Medicine Mountain by the Pikuni (Black-foot) tribe, after the bear's hump appearance of the spur that the trail ascends. After reaching the first bench, the climb levels off a bit, then steepens to a veritable staircase up the mountainside. The climb increases further after the second rest bench, and aerial views of the Prince of Wales Hotel with its solitary spire can be seen to the south.

The climb ends atop the rocky dome of the Bears Hump. Spectacular views stretch in all directions, high-lighted by the sapphire waters of Waterton Lake stretching southward into the United States. From north to south, the rugged crags rising above its far shore are Vimy Peak, Mount Boswell, and Mount Cleveland, which is the tallest summit in either national park at 10,466 feet. Mount Richard is the most prominent peak on the eastern shore of the lake, and in the distance is the jagged jawbone of the Citadel Peaks,

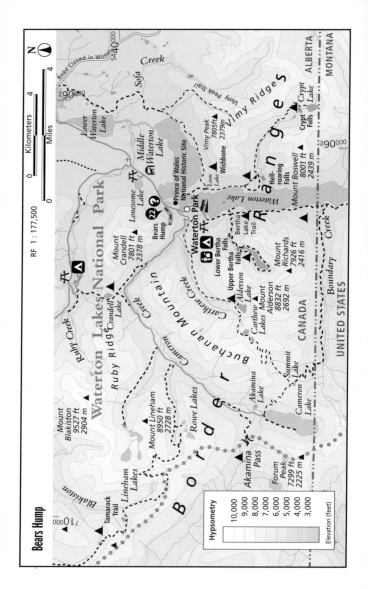

known as *Ataniawxis,* or "The Needles," to the Pikuni people. Looking west, views up Carthew Creek feature the rocky summit of Buchanan Peak. And to the east, the Waterton River wanders out onto the verdant grasslands of the high plains.

Key Points

0.0 Trail sign.
0.9 Trail ends atop Bears Hump.
1.8 Return to trailhead.

23 Lower Bertha Falls

Type of hike: Out-and-back
Total distance: 3.8 miles (6.1 km) round-trip

Time required: 2 to 3.5 hours
Elevation change: 700-foot gain

Finding the trailhead: The trail begins in the southwest corner of Waterton townsite, across from the automobile campground. The trailhead is marked by a sign for Bertha Lake and has its own parking lot.

The Hike

This popular day hike along Waterton Lake offers interpretive signs along the route, explaining the ecology of the ever–changing forest. At the end of the trek is the graceful veil of Lower Bertha Falls.

The trail begins in a stand of aspens, climbing gradually as it follows the western shore of Waterton Lake. As the trail

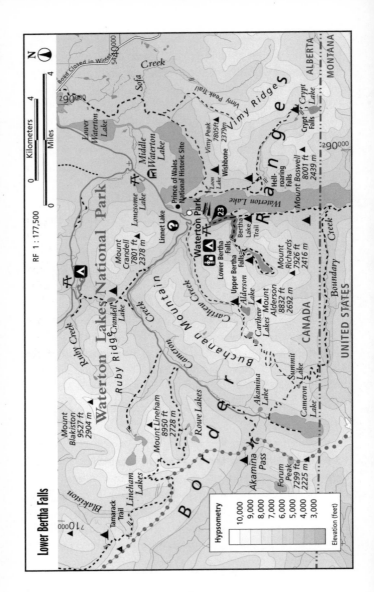

Lower Bertha Falls

RF 1 : 177,500

N

Kilometers
0   4
Miles
0   4

Waterton Lakes National Park

Ruby Creek

Mount Blakiston
9527 ft
2904 m

Tamarack Trail

Blakiston

Lineham Lakes

Mount Lineham
8950 ft
2728 m

Rowe Lakes

Akamina Pass

Forum Peak
7299 ft
2225 m

B o r d e r

Akamina Lake

Summit Lake

Cameron Lake

Lineham Creek

Cameron Creek

Ruby Ridge

Crandell Lake

Mount Crandell
7801 ft
2378 m

Lonesome Lake

Linnet Lake

Buchanan Mountain

Carthew Creek

Carthew Lakes

Mount Alderson
8832 ft
2692 m

Alderson Lake

Upper Bertha Falls

Lower Bertha Falls

Waterton Park

Mount Richards
7926 ft
2416 m

Bertha Lake

Bertha Trail

Mount Boswell
8001 ft
2439 m

Hell-roaring Falls

Prince of Wales National Historic Site

Middle Waterton Lake

Lower Waterton Lake

Waterton Lake

Leon Lake

Wishbone

Vimy Peak
7805 ft
2379 m

Vimy Peak Trail

Sofa Creek

V i m y   R i d g e s

R a n g e s

Crypt Falls

Crypt Lake

ALBERTA

MONTANA

CANADA

UNITED STATES

Boundary Creek

Road Closed in Winter

710 000

290 000

540 000

Hypsometry

Elevation (feet)
10,000
9,000
8,000
7,000
6,000
5,000
4,000
3,000

rises above the lakeshore, it crosses a mixed forest of lodge-pole pine, fir, and mountain maple. Rocky outcrops are home to limber pine, which thrives in extreme environments. An overlook about 1 mile (1.7 km) down the trail offers sweeping views of the ranges east of the lake, as far south as Mount Cleveland across the international border. At 10,466 feet above sea level, this summit is the loftiest in either park.

Just beyond this overlook, the Bertha Lake Trail splits off from the main trail that runs along the shores of Waterton Lake. A left turn here yields a steep 0.5-mile (1-km) descent to the Bertha Bay Campground. Turn right on the Bertha Lake Trail. It bends west, entering the beargrass-studded Bertha Creek Valley. After a distance of a mile, the trail reaches the foot of Lower Bertha Falls. Here, Bertha Creek cascades across layers of resistant rock, tumbling into a rushing flume created by a joint in the bedrock. This spot is a nice place for a picnic and marks the end of the easy day hike. Ambitious travelers can continue up the trail another 1.6 miles (2.6 km) and 780 feet (245 m) to reach the shore of Bertha Lake.

Key Points

0.0   Trail sign.
0.9   Junction with Waterton Lake Trail. Stay right for Bertha Lake.
1.9   Lower Bertha Falls. End of self-guiding nature trail.
3.8   Return to trailhead.

24 Rainbow Falls

Type of hike: Out-and-back
Total distance: 1.4 miles (2.3 km) round-trip

Time required: 45 minutes to 1.5 hours
Elevation change: Minimal

Finding the trailhead: The trail starts at Goat Haunt Ranger Station, reached by ferry from Waterton townsite or by trail along the western shore of Waterton Lake. The trailhead is located next to the stables, south of the ranger station.

The Hike

This well-maintained trail is a popular stroll for visitors who take the boat tour to the head of Waterton Lake. The hike begins on the Waterton Lake Trail, which runs westward from Goat Haunt Ranger Station. Barren summits of sedimentary rock flank both sides of Waterton Lake. As the trail nears the Waterton River, bear left on the hiker trail, then turn left at a marked junction with the Rainbow Falls spur trail. This path wanders up the east bank of the river, which is bordered by dense thickets of willow, a favorite winter forage of moose. After 0.5 mile, the trail reaches Rainbow Falls. Here, the translucent waters of the river foam over a series of low waterfalls.

Key Points

0.0 Trail sign behind stables. Follow Waterton Lake Trail.

0.2 Junction with Rainbow Falls spur on near bank of Waterton River. Turn left.

0.7 Rainbow Falls.

1.4 Return to trailhead.

Rainbow Falls

RF 1:177,500

Kilometers

Miles

N

Hypsometry

10,000
9,000
8,000
7,000
6,000
5,000
4,000
3,000

Elevation (feet)

Carthew Creek

Visitor Reception Centre

Middle Waterton Lake

Waterton Park

Loon Lake

Lower Bertha Falls

Upper Bertha Falls

Upper Waterton Lake

Vimy Ridge

Mount Alderson
8832 ft
2692 m

Bertha Lake

Hell-roaring Falls

B o r d e r

Mount Boswell
8001 ft
2439 m

Crypt Falls

Crypt Lake

CANADA

Boundary   Creek

R a n g e s

UNITED STATES

5430 000

Campbell Mountain
8245 ft
2513 m

Waterton Lake

Mount Olson
7913 ft
2412 m

Janet Lake

Goat Haunt Overlook

24

Goat Haunt

Goat Haunt Mountain
8641 ft
2634 m

Miche Wabun Lakes

Rainbow Falls

Olson   Creek

Waterton Valley Trail

Miche Wabun Glacier

P o r c u p i n e

R i d g e

Kootenai Lakes

Mount Cleveland
10466 ft
3190 m

Whitecrow Glacier

Stoney Indian Pass Trail

Valentine   Creek

5420 000

Glenns Lake

Kootenai Peak
8542 ft
2603 m

5420 000

Stoney Indian Lake

Stoney Indian Pass

Mokowanis Lake

Shepard Glacier

Sue Lake

Margaret Lake

Waterton Valley River

Chaney Glacier

Ipasha Lake

25 Kootenai Lakes

Type of hike: Out-and-back
Total distance: 5.6 miles (9 km)
round-trip

Time required: 3 to 5 hours
Elevation change: 200-foot gain

Finding the trailhead: Goat Haunt Ranger Station, reached by ferry from Waterton townsite or by trail along the western shore of Waterton Lake. The trailhead is located next to the stables, south of the ranger station.

The Hike

This long day hike follows the Waterton Valley Trail up the Waterton River from Goat Haunt Ranger Station, at the head of Waterton Lake. Hikers who attempt this route should catch a boat shuttle early in the morning in order to complete the trip before the last boat of the day departs for Waterton township. Kootenai Lakes provide fishing for good-size brook trout and the possibility of sighting moose. The lakes also offer backcountry campsites.

After leaving the paved walkways and buildings of the ranger station behind, the trail passes beneath a canopy of large old-growth conifers interrupted by occasional wet meadows. At mile 2.5, hikers reach a junction with the Kootenai Lakes Trail, which runs 0.3 mile westward to a campground at the foot of the lower lake. These shallow lakes provide good fishing for large brook trout, and the willows that crowd the shores provide a favored food source for moose, frequently seen here. Forested areas surrounding the lakes are prime habitat for black bears. The lakes are guarded to the west by the Citadel Peaks, the rocky spires at the tail end of Porcupine Ridge.

Kootenai Lakes

RF 1:177,500

Kilometers 0 ... 4

Miles 0 ... 4

N

Carthew Creek

Visitor Reception Centre

Middle Waterton Lake

Waterton Park

Loon Lake

Lower Bertha Falls

Upper Bertha Falls

Upper Waterton Lake

Vimy Ridge

Bertha Lake

Mount Alderson 8832 ft 2692 m

Hell-Roaring Falls

Hypsometry

10,000
9,000
8,000
7,000
6,000
5,000
4,000
3,000

Elevation (feet)

B o r d e r

Mount Boswell 8001 ft 2439 m

Crypt Falls

Crypt Lake

CANADA

Boundary Creek

UNITED STATES

R a n g e s

5430000

Waterton Lake

Campbell Mountain 8245 ft 2513 m

Mount Olson 7913 ft 2412 m

Janet Lake

Goat Haunt Overlook

25

Goat Haunt

Goat Haunt Mountain 8641 ft 2634 m

Miche Wabun Lakes

Kaina Mountain 9489 ft 2892 m

Rainbow Falls

Miche Wabun Glacier

Olson Creek

P o r c u p i n e   R i d g e

Waterton Valley Trail

Mount Cleveland 10466 ft 3190 m

Whitecrow Glacier

Stoney Indian Pass Trail

5420000

Kootenai Lakes

Valentine Creek

Glenns Lake

Kootenai Peak 8542 ft 2603 m

Stoney Indian Lake

Mokowanis Lake

Stoney Indian Pass

Shepard Glacier

Sue Lake

Margaret Lake

Waterton Valley River

Chaney Glacier

Ipasha Lake

Key Points

- **0.0** Trail sign. Trail follows the Waterton Valley floor.
- **2.5** Junction with Kootenai Lakes Trail. Turn right.
- **2.8** Kootenai Lakes.
- **5.6** Return to trailhead.

26 Cameron Lake

Type of hike: Out-and-back
Total distance: 2.2 miles (3.5 km) round-trip

Time required: 1 hour
Elevation change: Minimal

Finding the trailhead: Follow the paved Cameron Lake Road all the way to its end. The trail starts from a signpost in the lakeshore picnic area.

The Hike

This trail runs along the western shore of Cameron Lake, one of the prettiest lakes in the Waterton–Glacier area. A self-guiding pamphlet, available at the trailhead, interprets the ecology of the subalpine forest found along the lake.

From the picnic area, the trail runs through the spruce and fir woodland beside the lake, climbing and falling moderately. As it nears the head of the lake, the trail seeks out a small point where avalanches from Forum Peak have cleared away the trees. Here, hikers get outstanding views of the spectacular Mount Custer headwall and the deep turquoise waters of the lake.

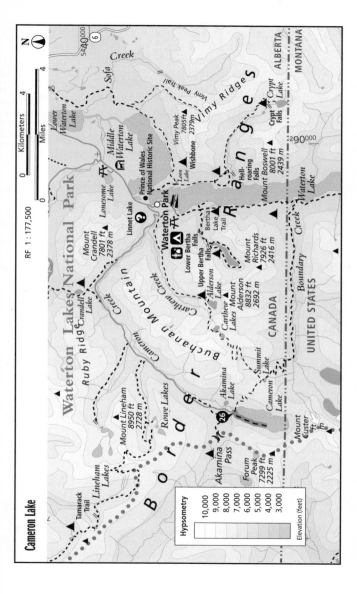

Cameron Lake

RF 1 : 177,500

N

0 ___ Kilometers ___ 4

0 ___ Miles ___ 4

Hypsometry

| 10,000 |
| 9,000 |
| 8,000 |
| 7,000 |
| 6,000 |
| 5,000 |
| 4,000 |
| 3,000 |

Elevation (feet)

540 000

6

Sofa   *Creek*

Lower Waterton Lake

Middle Waterton Lake

Waterton National Historic Site

Prince of Wales National Historic Site

Vimy Peak Trail

Vimy Peak 7805 ft 2379 m

Wishbone

Loon Lake

V   i   m   y   R   i   d   g   e   s

R   a   n   g   e   s

Hell-roaring Falls

Mount Boswell 8001 ft 2439 m

Crypt Falls

Crypt Lake

290 000

ALBERTA

MONTANA

Waterton Lake

Waterton Lakes National Park

Mount Crandell 7801 ft 2378 m

Lonesome Lake

Linnet Lake

Waterton Park

Lower Bertha Falls

Upper Bertha Falls

Bertha Trail

Bertha Lake

Alderson Lake

Carthew Creek

Mount Richards 7926 ft 2416 m

Ruby Ridge

Crandell Lake

Crandell Creek

Buchanan Mountain

Cameron Creek

Carthew Lakes

Mount Alderson 8832 ft 2692 m

CANADA

UNITED STATES

Boundary Creek

Waterton Creek

Mount Lineham 8950 ft 2728 m

Lineham Lakes

Tamarack Trail

Rowe Lakes

B   o   r   d   e   r

Akamina Pass

26

Akamina Lake

Summit Lake

Cameron Lake

Forum Peak 7299 ft 2225 m

Mount Custer ___ ft ___ m

27 Lineham Falls

Type of hike: Out-and-back
Total distance: 5.2 miles (8.4
km) round-trip

Time required: 2.5 to 4 hours
Elevation change: 1,290-foot
gain, 130-foot loss

Finding the trailhead: The trail begins at a marked pullout on the
north side of the Cameron Lake Road, just beyond the historic oil well
site.

The Hike

This pleasant jaunt runs up Lineham Creek to a headwall
that rises below a high lake basin. A trail once climbed the
headwall with the assistance of cable handrails, but that route
has long since been abandoned. The headwall rock is loose
and crumbly, and is considered hazardous even by experi-
enced climbers; travelers should not attempt to reach Lineham Lakes via this route.

From the trailhead, our trail takes travelers across wooded
flats populated by lodgepole pine and aspen. About 0.25 mile
from the road, a steady ascent through the forest takes hikers
onto the shoulders of Ruby Ridge as the trail runs westward, high above Lineham Creek. The forest gives way to
grassy slopes, and the trail continues to climb as Mount
Lineham rises like a lone sentinel across the valley. A back-
ward glance reveals the massive peaks of Buchanan Ridge,
which block out the skyline to the east. A mile farther on,
the trail enters a forest of tall fir trees and begins to level out.
Views are limited to brief glimpses through openings in the
forest canopy as the trail tracks west across the soft duff of
the forest floor.

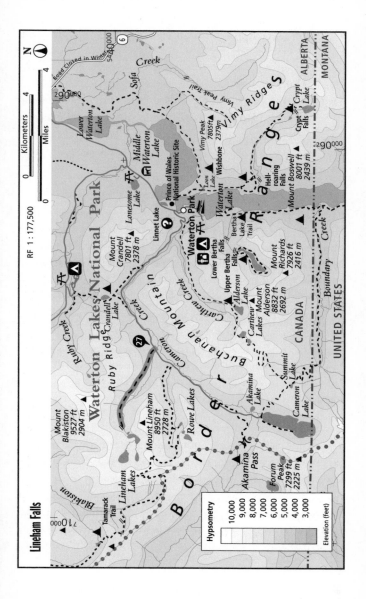

Upon entering a broad avalanche path that descends from the rocky face of Mount Blakiston, the trail switchbacks downward about 100 feet to reach the level of the creek. The path meanders beside the stream, which tumbles down a series of cheerful cascades within a narrow canyon. When the trail runs out onto alpine meadows to reach its official terminus, a spur trail runs down to the creek for a clear view of 410-foot Lineham Falls, while a higher path runs uphill for a loftier perspective.

28 Blakiston Falls

Type of hike: Out-and-back
Total distance: 1.6 miles (2.6 km) round-trip

Time required: 45 minutes to 1.5 hours
Elevation change: Minimal

Finding the trailhead: The trail begins from the Red Rock Canyon parking lot. Cross Red Rock Creek and take a left to descend to the bridge over Bauerman Creek, which is the starting point for the Blakiston Trail.

The Hike

From the parking lot at Red Rock Canyon, cross Red Rock Creek and turn left, descending along its northwest bank to reach a stout bridge above Bauerman Creek. Mount Blakiston rises to the south, while Anderson Peak is to the west. Once across this bridge, take the rightmost trail, which is for hikers. The trail climbs gently through coniferous forest, with views of Mount Blakiston through numerous openings. At Blakiston Falls, the trail passes a wooden observation

Blakiston Falls

RF 1 : 177,500

N

Waterton Lakes National Park

Galwey Brook

Horseshoe Basin

Crandell Mountain

Red Rock Canyon

Road Closed in Winter

Blakiston Creek

Blakiston Falls

28

Anderson Peak
8851 ft
2698 m

Lost Mountain Peak
8230 ft
2509 m

Bauerman Creek

Avion Ridge

Avion Ridge

7000000

Lost Lake Trail

Twin Lakes

Sage Pass

Kishinena Peak

South Kootenai Pass

Clark

Lone Mountain
7939 ft
2420 m

Blakiston Valley Trail

Blakiston Creek

Blakiston

Mount Blakiston
9527 ft
2904 m

Range

Lineham Lakes

Festubert Mountain

Mount Lineham
8950 ft
2728 m

Rowe Lakes

Ruby Ridge

Crandell Lake

Crandell Creek

Buchanan Mountain

Cameron Creek

Mount Crandell
7801 ft
2378 m

Lonesome Lake

Linnet Lake

Middle Waterton

Waterton

Prince of Wales National Historic Site

Upper Waterton Lake

Waterton Park

UTM Zone 12
UTM Zone 11

5440000

5440000

710000

290000

290000

0   2   4 Kilometers

0   2   4 Miles

Hypsometry

10,000
9,000
8,000
7,000
6,000
5,000
4,000
3,000

Elevation (feet)

platform that leans out over the water to provide excellent views of the thundering cascade.

Key Points

0.0 Trail sign. Take the paved trail across Red Rock Creek, then turn left.

0.2 Bridge over Bauerman Creek.

0.8 Blakiston Falls.

1.6 Return to trailhead.

Index

About The Author

Erik Molvar discovered backpacking while working on a volunteer trail crew in the North Cascades of Washington. A newfound taste for the wilderness experience inspired him to choose a career in the outdoors, and he soon found himself at the University of Montana pursuing a bachelor's degree in wildlife biology. Montana's craggy ranges were to be his weekend playground for the next five years, and two summers of bartending at Lake McDonald Lodge gave Erik the perfect opportunity to fully explore Glacier National Park's backcountry. An adventurous spirit has led Erik to embark upon backpacking expeditions throughout the Rocky Mountains, the Great Basin, western Canada, and Alaska. After studying moose behavior in Alaska on the way to a master's degree, Erik is now executive director of Biodiversity Conservation Alliance, one of the most effective nonprofit conservation organizations in the West. Other books by the author: *Hiking the North Cascades, Best Easy Day Hikes North Cascades, Hiking Olympic National Park, Best Easy Day Hikes Olympics, Hiking Glacier and Waterton Lakes National Parks, Hiking Montana's Bob Marshall Wilderness, Wild Wyoming, Hiking Wyoming's Cloud Peak Wilderness, Hiking Colorado's Maroon Bells–Snowmass Wilderness, Hiking Arizona's Cactus Country, Hiking Zion and Bryce Canyon National Parks, Alaska on Foot: Wilderness Techniques for the Far North,* and *Scenic Driving Alaska and the Yukon.*